THE XXL UK CROCKPOT COOKBOOK

1600 Days of Weeknight and Family-Friendly Crockpot Recipes Using the Metric Measurements and Local No-Fuss Ingredients to Make Dinner Easy

Renee R. Legere

Copyright© 2024 By Renee R. Legere Rights Reserved

This book is copyright protected. It is only for personal use. You cannot amend, distribute, sell, use, quote or paraphrase any part of the content within this book, without the consent of the author or publisher.

Under no circumstances will any blame or legal responsibility be held against the publisher, or author, for any damages, reparation, or monetary loss due to the information contained within this book, either directly or indirectly.

Limit of Liability/Disclaimer of Warranty:

No book, including this one, can ever replace the diagnostic expertise and medical advice of a physician in providing information about your health. The information contained herein is not intended to replace medical advice. You should consult with your doctor before using the information in this or any health-related book.

The Publisher and the author make no representations or warranties with respect to the accuracy or completeness of the contents of this work and specifically disclaim all warranties, including without limitation warranties of fitness for a particular purpose. No warranty may be created or extended by sales or promotional materials. The advice and strategies contained herein may not be suitable for every situation. This work is sold with the understanding that the Publisher is not engaged in rendering medical, legal, or other professional advice or services. If professional assistance is required, the services of a competent professional person should be sought. Neither the Publisher nor the author shall be liable for damages arising here from. The fact that an individual, organization, or website is referred to in this work as a citation and/or potential source of further information does not mean that the author or the Publisher endorses the information the individual, organization, or website may provide or recommendations they/it may make. Further, readers should be aware that websites listed in this work may have changed or disappeared between when this work was written and when it is read.

Manufactured in the United Kingdom
Interior and Cover Designer: Danielle Rees
Art Producer: Brooke White
Editor: Aaliyah Lyons
Production Editor: Sienna Adams
Production Manager: Sarah Johnson
Photography: Michael Smith

TABLE OF CONTENTS

Introduction 1

Chapter 1: The Evolution of Crockpot Cuisine 2

    How the Crockpot Works 2

    Benefits of Crockpot Cooking 3

    Tips for Using Your Crockpot 4

Chapter 2: Appetizers and Snacks 6

    Easy Mexican-Style Cheese Dip 7

    Cider and Cheese Fondue 7

    Mediterranean Artichoke and Pepper Spread 7

    Hot Crab Dip 7

    Broccoli and Cheese Dip 8

    Mediterranean Artichoke Dip 8

    Creamy Dauphinoise Potatoes 8

    Cheesy Hash Browns 9

    Traditional Apple Butter 9

    Toffee Apple Dip 9

    Light Spinach and Leek Dip 9

    Cheesy Salsa Dip 10

    Pickled White Fish 10

    Sweet and Tangy Cocktail Sausages 10

    Creamy Polenta 10

    Blueberry Bread and Butter Pudding 11

    Spiced Apple Butter 11

    Keto-Friendly Granola 11

    Star Anise Apple Butter 12

    Savoury Party Mix 12

    Crunchy Cereal Snack Mix 12

TABLE OF CONTENTS

    Rich Hot Chocolate 12

Chapter 3: Breakfasts and Brunches 13

    Crockpot Porridge 14

    Breakfast Fruit Compote 14

    Traditional Boston Brown Bread 14

    Keto Breakfast Bowl 15

    Pumpkin and Pecan Porridge 15

    Tropical Baked Porridge 15

    Cinnamon Streusel Cake 15

    Pulled BBQ Beef Rolls 16

    Cheesy Polenta with Green Chillies 16

    Sausage and Cheese Breakfast Strata 16

    Simple Hominy Porridge 17

    Spiced Pear Porridge 17

    Leek, Bacon and Goat's Cheese Strata 17

    Spiced Breakfast Prunes 18

    Apple and Blueberry Compote 18

    Mediterranean Vegetable Hash with Eggs 18

    Traditional Porridge 19

    Cherry and Quinoa Porridge 19

    Beetroot Hash with Poached Eggs 19

    Spiced Sweet Potato Hash 20

    Festive Morning Punch 20

    Courgette and Mushroom Breakfast Bake 20

Chapter 4: Poultry 21

    Greek-Style Chicken Pitta Filling 22

    Mexican Green Chilli Chicken Wraps 22

    Garlic Braised Chicken Thighs 22

    Japanese Teriyaki Chicken 22

TABLE OF CONTENTS

Creamy Mushroom Chicken 23

Chicken in Rich Bacon Gravy 23

Spicy Chicken Lettuce Wraps 23

Italian-Style Chicken Sausages with Beans 23

Mediterranean Chicken with Tomatoes and Olives 24

Poussin with Root Vegetables 24

Chicken and Prawn Rice 24

Quick Chicken Soup 24

Bacon and Feta-Stuffed Chicken 25

Chicken and Sage Stuffing Bake 25

Italian-Style Braised Turkey Sausages 25

Spicy Chicken with Rice 26

Chicken, Broccoli and Rice Bake 26

Mediterranean Chicken Rolls 26

Chicken with Mushrooms and Shallots 27

Asian Chicken Ginger 27

Italian Chicken Stew 27

Chapter 5: Red Meats 28

Fruited Pork 29

Apple and Cranberry Pork 29

Italian-Style Roast with Potatoes 29

Ginger Beef 30

Balsamic Beef with Red Cabbage 30

Emergency Frozen Roast Beef 30

Traditional Pork and Sauerkraut 31

Autumn Harvest Pork Loin 31

Beef Ribs 31

Pork Chops in Tomato Sauce 31

Tex-Mex Beef 32

Sweet and Savory Brisket 32

TABLE OF CONTENTS

Sausage and Vegetable Casserole 32
Pulled Pork in BBQ Sauce 32
Spicy Shredded Beef Rolls 33
Tender Pork Joint 33
Korean-Style Pulled Pork with Kimchi 33
Pork Joint with Potatoes and Onions 33
BBQ-Style Beef Joint 34
Orange and Cranberry Pork Joint 34
Spiced Pork Tacos with Mole Sauce 34
Ham and Cheese Pasta Bake 35
Herbed Pork Fillets 35
Cheesy Ham and Mash Bake 35
Sauerkraut with Two Meats 36
Beef and Gravy 36
Herbed Pork Fillet with Mediterranean Vegetables 36

Chapter 6: Fish and Seafood 37

Soy-Ginger Steamed Fish 38
Tuna and Pasta Bake 38
Cajun Prawns with Grits 38
Creamy Tuna Pasta Bake 38
Chicken and Prawn Jambalaya 39
Italian Fish Stew 39
Tuna and Stuffing Loaf 39
Lemon and Dill Salmon 39
Crab Pasta Sauce 40
Mediterranean-Style Cod 40
Spicy Prawn Tacos 40
Classic Fish Stew 40
Coconut and Lime Prawn Curry 41
Wine-Poached Salmon 41

TABLE OF CONTENTS

Thai Coconut Seafood Soup 41

Garlic and Herb Butter Prawns 41

Teriyaki Salmon 42

Courgette and Prawn Gratin 42

Moroccan Fish Tagine 42

Lime Cod and Prawns 43

Mussels in Cream 43

Seafood Jambalaya 43

Soy and Ginger Braised Squid 43

Chocolate and Crispy Bacon Cupcakes 44

Herb-Crusted Flounder 44

Chapter 7: Soups and Stew 45

Cheesy Bacon and Cauliflower Soup 46

Quick Minced Beef and Vegetable Soup 46

Classic Beef and Vegetable Soup 46

Pizza Soup 46

Simple Vegetable and Mince Soup 47

Cheddar Cheese and Vegetable Soup 47

Creamy Beef and Vegetable Soup 47

Pizza-Style Taco Soup 47

Potato and Spinach Soup 48

Spicy Italian Sausage and Potato Soup 48

Mixed Bean and Sausage Stew 48

French Country Bean Soup 48

Spicy Bean Soup 49

Black Bean and Pork Chilli 49

Minced Beef and Polish Sausage Soup 49

Lentil and Vegetable Soup 49

Tuscan Sausage and Potato Soup 50

Rustic Bean and Bacon Soup 50

TABLE OF CONTENTS

Country Bean and Ham Soup 50

Chapter 8: Vegan and Vegetarian 51

Convenient Crockpot Lasagna 52

Lentil Ragu with Pasta 52

Indian-Style Vegetable Curry 52

Vegetarian Sloppy Joes 53

Traditional Beef Borscht 53

Creamed Spinach Bake 53

Mediterranean Brussels Sprouts 53

Creamy Broccoli and Cauliflower Bake 54

Classic Macaroni Cheese 54

Wild Rice with Bacon and Cherries 54

Lemon and Herb Pearl Barley 54

Sweet and Sour Spiced Cabbage 55

Rich Two-Cheese Macaroni 55

Quinoa, Black Bean and Mango Salad 55

Orange-Glazed Baby Carrots 56

Navy Bean and Bacon Soup 56

Light Macaroni Cheese 56

Cheesy Pizza Pasta 56

Cheese and Bread Soufflé 57

Spanish Rice with Black Beans 57

Summer Pearl Barley Salad 57

Tempeh-Stuffed Peppers 58

Quinoa-Stuffed Onions 58

Braised Swiss Chard with Shiitake Mushrooms 58

Creamy Spaghetti with Minced Beef 59

Cheesy Cabbage Casserole 59

Vegetarian Lasagne 59

TABLE OF CONTENTS

Chapter 9: Desserts 60

    Chocolate Peanut Butter Sponge 61

    Simple Stuffed Apples 61

    Vanilla Pod Rice Pudding 61

    Apple Crumble 62

    Lemon and Poppy Seed Drizzle Pudding 62

    Seven Layer Traybake 62

    Strawberry and Rhubarb Compote 62

    Toffee Apples 63

    Lemon Rice Pudding 63

    White Wine Poached Pears 63

    Double Chocolate Bread and Butter Pudding 63

    Chocolate Pots de Crème 64

    Spiced Fruit Compote 64

    Tea-Poached Pears 64

    Rum-Glazed Bananas 65

    Apple and Caramel Pudding 65

    Scandinavian Fruit Compote 65

    Butterscotch Apple Crumble 65

    Spiced Fruit Sauce 66

    Fruit and Nut Stuffed Apples 66

    Chocolate Self-Saucing Pudding 66

Appendix 1: Measurement Conversion Chart 67

Appendix 2: The Dirty Dozen and Clean Fifteen 68

Appendix 3: Index 69

INTRODUCTION

As a busy mum juggling work, school runs, and everything in between, I've always dreamt of a magical solution to dinnertime chaos. A few years ago, my husband, Oliver, gifted me a crockpot for my birthday. At first, I wasn't sure what to make of it—was it just another kitchen gadget destined to gather dust? Oh, how wrong I was.

One cold winter's evening, with a mountain of laundry and homework to tackle, I decided to give it a go. I tossed in some chicken thighs, root vegetables, and a medley of herbs, poured over some stock, and switched it on. By dinnertime, the house was filled with the most heavenly aroma. My family gathered around the table, their faces lighting up as I ladled the tender, flavourful stew into bowls. That was the moment I knew the crockpot wasn't just a gadget—it was a lifesaver.

Since then, it's been my secret weapon. Whether it's a hearty soup bubbling away while I'm out running errands or a slow-cooked curry ready when we return from football practice, the crockpot has transformed our mealtimes. It's not just about convenience—it's about nourishing my family with wholesome, home-cooked meals.

I've even discovered how versatile it can be, experimenting with everything from casseroles to desserts. The best part? The crockpot does all the hard work, leaving me more time to enjoy with my loved ones. It's given me peace of mind knowing that, even on the busiest days, a delicious, healthy meal is always waiting.

For me, the crockpot isn't just a kitchen appliance; it's a little piece of sanity wrapped in a warm, comforting embrace. I honestly don't know how I managed before it.

DEDICATION

To Oliver, every day with you feels like a gift, but it's the little moments we share that mean the most to me. From bustling around the kitchen together, laughing over silly mishaps, to sitting down to enjoy the meals we've created, you've turned ordinary routines into extraordinary memories. Cooking with you has brought so much warmth and joy to my life—it's more than just making food; it's about creating love and comfort for our family. Thank you for being my partner in life and in the kitchen. Here's to many more meals and happy moments together.

CHAPTER 1: THE EVOLUTION OF CROCKPOT CUISINE

HOW THE CROCKPOT WORKS

The Crockpot, a humble kitchen appliance, has earned its place as an indispensable tool for modern home cooks, transforming raw ingredients into delectable meals through the gentle alchemy of slow cooking. Understanding how the Crockpot works involves unraveling the science behind its seemingly magical ability to turn simple ingredients into flavorful masterpieces.

At the heart of the Crockpot's functionality is the concept of slow cooking, a method that harnesses low heat over an extended period to break down tough cuts of meat, infuse flavors, and meld ingredients into a harmonious symphony of tastes and textures. The Crockpot achieves this through a combination of time, temperature, and a sealed cooking environment.

LOW AND SLOW TEMPERATURE CONTROL:

The Crockpot operates at low temperatures, typically between 77°C to 138°C. This deliberate choice of low heat serves two essential purposes.

First, it prevents the rapid breakdown of proteins, ensuring that meats remain tender and succulent rather than becoming tough and dry. Second, it allows the gradual release of flavors from herbs, spices, and other ingredients, resulting in a deeply infused, aromatic dish.

The slow cooking process also has the advantage of minimizing the risk of overcooking. With high temperatures, there is a higher chance of ingredients becoming dry or losing their structural integrity. The low and slow approach ensures a gradual and controlled transformation, resulting in dishes that are consistently flavorful and perfectly cooked.

SEALED COOKING ENVIRONMENT:

One key feature of the Crockpot is its sealed cooking environment. The tightly sealed lid traps moisture within the pot, preventing it from evaporating into the air. This moisture, in the form of steam, circulates within the pot, creating a self-basting effect. As the ingredients release their natural juices, they mix and mingle, enhancing the overall depth of flavor.

The sealed environment also contributes to the even distribution of heat. Every corner of the pot experiences the same gentle warmth, ensuring that each ingredient receives equal attention. This eliminates the need for constant stirring and allows for a hands-off cooking experience, making the Crockpot an ideal companion for busy individuals seeking a convenient yet delicious meal solution.

BREAKING DOWN TOUGH FIBERS:

The Crockpot excels at transforming tougher cuts of meat into melt-in-your-mouth delicacies. Collagen, a connective tissue found in meat, breaks down into gelatin during slow cooking. This process occurs at low temperatures over an extended period, resulting in meats that are not only tender but also imbued with a rich, silky mouthfeel.

The breakdown of tough fibers is not limited to meat alone; it extends to vegetables and legumes, rendering them soft and flavorful. The slow, steady application of heat allows for a thorough breakdown of complex carbohydrates and fibers, unlocking the full potential of each ingredient.

FLAVOR DEVELOPMENT AND INFUSION:

The extended cooking time in the Crockpot facilitates the gradual release and melding of flavors. Spices, herbs, and aromatic ingredients have ample time to impart their essence to the dish, creating a depth of flavor that distinguishes slow-cooked meals. The result is a symphony of tastes where each ingredient contributes its unique notes, resulting in a harmonious and well-balanced final product.

BENEFITS OF CROCKPOT COOKING

As more home cooks discover the advantages of incorporating a Crockpot into their routine, they not only find themselves with more free time but also enjoy enhanced flavors, improved nutrition, and a simplified cooking experience.

TIME EFFICIENCY:

One of the most celebrated benefits of Crockpot cooking is its time efficiency. In a world where time is a precious commodity, the Crockpot becomes a culinary ally by allowing busy individuals to prepare delicious, homemade meals with minimal hands-on time. The slow cooking process takes place over several hours, often while individuals are at work or engaged in other activities, eliminating the need for constant monitoring. This results in a hot, flavorful meal waiting at home, ready to be enjoyed at the end of a hectic day.

ENHANCED FLAVORS:

The slow and steady approach to cooking in a Crockpot works wonders for flavor development. As ingredients simmer in their own juices, spices, and herbs over an extended period, the result is a depth of flavor that is unparalleled. The sealed cooking environment helps to retain and circulate moisture, intensifying the taste and aroma of each ingredient. Meats become tender and succulent, while vegetables absorb the rich essence of the dish. The result is a flavorful masterpiece that tantalizes the taste buds and satisfies the senses.

NUTRIENT RETENTION:

Contrary to the misconception that slow cooking might compromise the nutritional content of food, Crockpots excel at preserving the goodness in ingredients. The low and slow cooking process minimizes nutrient loss, especially when compared to more rapid cooking methods. Vitamins and minerals present in vegetables and meats are

CHAPTER 1

retained, ensuring that the final dish not only tastes delicious but also provides a wholesome and nutritious meal for the entire family.

COST-EFFECTIVE COOKING:

Crockpot cooking often involves less expensive cuts of meat that benefit from the slow cooking process. Tougher cuts, rich in flavor but traditionally requiring extended cooking times, become tender and succulent in the Crockpot. This not only allows for economic meal planning but also opens up a world of culinary possibilities, encouraging home cooks to experiment with a variety of ingredients without breaking the budget.

VERSATILITY IN MEAL PREPARATION:

The versatility of the Crockpot extends beyond traditional stews and casseroles. From soups and curries to desserts and breakfast dishes, the Crockpot can handle a wide array of recipes. Its adaptability enables home cooks to explore diverse cuisines and experiment with ingredients, providing a canvas for creative expression in the kitchen. This versatility is particularly advantageous for those seeking to diversify their menu without investing excessive time and effort.

SIMPLIFIED COOKING PROCESS:

Crockpot cooking simplifies the cooking process by minimizing the need for constant attention and elaborate preparation. The "set it and forget it" approach allows individuals to add ingredients to the pot, set the desired temperature, and carry on with their day. This simplicity not only reduces stress in the kitchen but also encourages individuals, including those with limited culinary expertise, to venture into home cooking with confidence.

ECONOMICAL ENERGY USAGE:

Crockpots are energy-efficient appliances. Their low-wattage design allows for extended cooking times without a significant impact on energy consumption. Compared to traditional ovens or stovetop cooking, the Crockpot proves to be an economical choice, contributing to reduced energy bills and a more sustainable approach to home cooking.

TIPS FOR USING YOUR CROCKPOT

The Crockpot, with its slow and steady approach to cooking, has become a kitchen essential for those seeking convenience without compromising on flavour. To ensure your Crockpot culinary adventures are a resounding success, consider the following detailed tips that will elevate your slow cooking experience.

Choose the Right Size: Selecting the appropriate Crockpot size is crucial. If your pot is too small, ingredients may not fit; if it's too large, your meal might not cook evenly. Consider the size of your household and the portion sizes you typically prepare when making your selection.

Layer Ingredients Wisely: For even cooking, strategically layer your ingredients. Place denser and slower-cooking items at the bottom and around the sides of the pot. This arrangement ensures uniform heat distribution, preventing some elements from overcooking while others remain undercooked.

Prep Ingredients Ahead of Time: To streamline your cooking process, prep ingredients in advance. Chop vegetables, trim meats, and measure spices before starting your Crockpot. This not only saves time during the cooking process but also ensures a smooth and stress-free preparation.

THE EVOLUTION OF CROCKPOT CUISINE

Sear Meats for Flavor: While not mandatory, searing meats before placing them in the Crockpot adds a layer of depth to the flavour profile. The browning process locks in juices and enhances the overall taste of your dish. If time allows, consider incorporating this extra step for a richer culinary experience.

Use the Right Temperature: Understanding temperature settings is crucial for successful Crockpot cooking. Most recipes will provide guidelines for low, medium, and high settings. Low heat is perfect for long cooking hours, while high heat accelerates the process. Adjust the temperature based on your desired cooking time and results.

Avoid the Temptation to Peek: Resist the urge to lift the lid frequently. Each time you do, heat escapes, potentially extending the cooking time. Trust the process, and only check on your meal when necessary to avoid disrupting the slow cooking magic happening inside.

Add Dairy Towards the End: Dairy products such as milk or cream can curdle if added too early in the cooking process. To maintain a creamy consistency, incorporate dairy-based ingredients during the final hour of cooking.

Adjust Seasoning at the End: Flavours intensify during slow cooking, and as a result, your dish might require less seasoning than initially thought. Taste and adjust the seasoning in the last hour of cooking to ensure a perfectly balanced flavour profile.

Utilize the Warm Setting: Once your meal is ready, switch the Crockpot to the warm setting. This ensures your dish remains at a safe temperature until you're ready to serve, making it convenient for those unpredictable dinner times.

Don't Overfill: To prevent uneven cooking and potential spillage, avoid filling the Crockpot to the brim. Leave some space for ingredients to expand as they cook, ensuring a mess-free and safe cooking experience.

Thicken Sauces if Needed: If your dish has too much liquid, you can create a slurry of flour or cornstarch mixed with water and stir it in during the last hour of cooking. This will help thicken the sauce to your desired consistency.

Clean with Ease: Many Crockpot inserts are removable and dishwasher safe. Before placing them in the dishwasher, check the manufacturer's instructions to ensure proper care. This feature simplifies the cleaning process, making the aftermath of your culinary adventure more

manageable.

Experiment with Flavors: The slow cooking process allows for the melding of flavours beautifully. Feel free to experiment with herbs, spices, and unique ingredient combinations. Use your Crockpot as a canvas for culinary creativity, and discover new and exciting flavour profiles.

Keep a Crockpot Cookbook Handy: Investing in a quality Crockpot cookbook can be a game-changer. It provides a wealth of inspiration, guiding you through diverse recipes and helping you unlock the full potential of your crockpot. Explore new cuisines, try different techniques, and make the most of your culinary journey.

Enjoy the Journey: Crockpot cooking is not just about the destination; it's about the journey. Embrace the convenience, enjoy the process, and savor the anticipation as your home fills with the delightful aroma of a slow-cooked masterpiece. This is not just cooking; it's an experience that brings joy and satisfaction to both the cook and those fortunate enough to enjoy the results.

CHAPTER 2: APPETIZERS AND SNACKS

APPETIZERS AND SNACKS

EASY MEXICAN-STYLE CHEESE DIP

Prep time: 15 minutes | Cook time: 2 hours | Serves 10-15

- 500g lean minced beef
- Pinch of salt
- Pinch of black pepper
- Pinch of onion powder
- 2 garlic cloves, finely chopped
- (optional)
- 2 × 450g jars of salsa, any heat level
- 400g tin refried beans
- 50g soured cream
- 300g grated mature Cheddar, divided

1. Brown the minced beef in a frying pan. Drain well. Season with salt, pepper, onion powder and chopped garlic.
2. Combine beef, salsa, beans, soured cream and 200g of the cheese in the crockpot.
3. Cover and cook on Low for 2 hours. Just before serving, sprinkle with remaining 100g cheese.
4. Serve with tortilla chips.

CIDER AND CHEESE FONDUE

Prep time: 15 minutes | Cook time: 1 hour | Serves 4

- 65ml dry cider (or apple juice for alcohol-free version)
- 200g grated mature Cheddar
- 100g grated Emmental cheese
- 1 tbsp cornflour
- ⅛ tsp black pepper
- 1 crusty baguette, cut into chunks

1. In a large saucepan, bring cider to the boil. Reduce heat to medium-low.
2. In a large bowl, toss both cheeses with cornflour and pepper.
3. Gradually stir cheese mixture into cider. Cook, stirring, for 3-4 minutes until cheese has melted.
4. Transfer to a 1-litre crockpot to keep warm. Stir occasionally.
5. Serve with bread chunks or apple wedges for dipping.

MEDITERRANEAN ARTICHOKE AND PEPPER SPREAD

Prep time: 10 minutes | Cook time: 1 hour | Makes 300g

- 100g freshly grated Parmesan
- 45g mayonnaise
- 20g full-fat soft cheese, at room temperature
- 1 garlic clove, finely chopped
- 400g tin artichoke hearts, drained and finely chopped
- 20g finely chopped roasted red peppers (from a jar)

1. In a food processor, combine Parmesan, mayonnaise, soft cheese and garlic. Blend until smooth. Transfer to crockpot.
2. Stir in artichoke hearts and red peppers until well combined.
3. Cover and cook on Low for 1 hour. Stir before serving.
4. Serve with crackers, crudités or crusty bread.

HOT CRAB DIP

Prep time: 15 minutes | Cook time: 3-4 hours | Makes 500g

- 20g salsa
- 45ml semi-skimmed milk
- 225g crab sticks, finely flaked
- 65g spring onions, thinly sliced
- 110g tinned green chillies, chopped
- 225g reduced-fat soft cheese, cubed
- Crackers to serve

1. Lightly grease the crockpot with cooking spray.
2. Mix salsa and milk in the crockpot.
3. Add all remaining ingredients except crackers.
4. Cover and cook on Low for 3-4 hours.
5. Stir every 30 minutes.
6. Serve with crackers or fresh vegetable crudités.

CHAPTER 2

BROCCOLI AND CHEESE DIP

Prep time: **15 minutes** | Cook time: **2 hours** | Makes **600g**

- 100g celery, finely chopped
- 45g onions, finely chopped
- 280g frozen chopped broccoli, cooked
- 100g cooked rice
- 295g tin reduced-fat cream of mushroom soup
- 450g jar reduced-fat cheese spread

1. Combine all ingredients in the crockpot.
2. Cover and cook on Low for 2 hours.
3. Serve with bread sticks or crackers.

MEDITERRANEAN ARTICHOKE DIP

Prep time: **10 minutes** | Cook time: **1-4 hours** | Makes **800g**

- 2 × 400g jars marinated artichoke hearts, drained
- 50g reduced-fat mayonnaise
- 50g reduced-fat soured cream
- 100g water chestnuts, chopped
- 20g freshly grated Parmesan
- 20g spring onions, finely chopped

1. Roughly chop artichoke hearts. Combine with mayonnaise, soured cream, water chestnuts, cheese and spring onions in the crockpot.
2. Cover and cook on High for 1-2 hours, or on Low for 3-4 hours.
3. Serve with crackers or crusty bread.

CREAMY DAUPHINOISE POTATOES

Prep time: **20 minutes** | Cook time: **7 hours** | Serves **9**

- Cooking spray
- 3 large Maris Piper potatoes, peeled and thinly sliced
- 1 onion, finely chopped
- 3 garlic cloves, finely chopped
- 1 tsp dried basil
- 1 tsp salt
- ⅛ tsp freshly ground black pepper
- 100g grated Havarti cheese
- 45g grated mature white Cheddar
- 45ml single cream
- 45ml double cream
- 30g butter
- 20g freshly grated Parmesan

1. Lightly coat the crockpot with cooking spray.
2. Layer potatoes, onion, garlic, basil, salt, pepper, Havarti and Cheddar in the crockpot, making approximately 4 layers.
3. In a small saucepan over high heat, warm both creams with butter until butter melts (about 1 minute). Pour over the layered ingredients and sprinkle with Parmesan.
4. Cover and cook on Low for 7 hours, or until potatoes are tender.

APPETIZERS AND SNACKS

CHEESY HASH BROWNS

Prep time: **10 minutes** | Cook time: **7 hours** | Serves **9**

- Cooking spray
- 570g frozen hash browns
- 1 onion, finely chopped
- 3 garlic cloves, finely chopped
- 100g grated Gruyère cheese (or mature Cheddar)
- 100ml whole milk
- 20ml double cream
- 45g butter
- ½ tsp dried marjoram
- ¼ tsp salt
- ⅛ tsp freshly ground black pepper
- 45g soured cream

1. Lightly coat the crockpot with cooking spray.
2. Combine hash browns, onion and garlic in the crockpot. Stir in the cheese.
3. In a small saucepan over high heat, combine milk, cream, butter, marjoram, salt and pepper. Heat until butter melts (about 1 minute). Remove from heat and stir in the soured cream.
4. Pour the milk mixture into the crockpot.
5. Cover and cook on Low for 7 hours, or until potatoes are tender.

TRADITIONAL APPLE BUTTER

Prep time: **15 minutes** | Cook time: **10-13 hours** | Makes **800g**

- 1.6kg Bramley apples (or other cooking apples)
- 200ml dry cider (or apple juice)
- 200g caster sugar
- 1 tsp ground cinnamon
- ⅛-¼ tsp ground cloves (start with ⅛ tsp, adjust to taste halfway through cooking)

1. Core and roughly chop the apples, leaving skins on. Combine apples and cider in the crockpot.
2. Cover and cook on Low for 9-12 hours, until apples have broken down and mixture has thickened.
3. Pass the mixture through a food mill or sieve.
4. Return purée to the crockpot.
5. Stir in sugar, cinnamon and cloves until well combined.
6. Cover and cook on Low for 1 hour.

TOFFEE APPLE DIP

Prep time: **15 minutes** | Cook time: **20 minutes** | Serves **24**

- 250g unsalted butter
- 200g soft light brown sugar
- 397g tin condensed milk
- 100g golden syrup
- 100g smooth peanut butter (optional)
- Selection of apple slices for dipping

1. Combine all ingredients except apples in a saucepan. Heat gently, stirring constantly, until smooth and just bubbling. Take care not to let it catch on the bottom.
2. Transfer to the crockpot.
3. Cover and cook on Low for 20 minutes.
4. Arrange apple slices on a serving plate.
5. Keep the dip warm in the crockpot on Low setting while serving.

LIGHT SPINACH AND LEEK DIP

Prep time: **10 minutes** | Cook time: **1 hour** | Makes **300g**

- 200g reduced-fat soured cream
- 20g light mayonnaise
- 280g frozen chopped spinach, thawed and well drained
- 1 packet dried leek soup mix
- 20g red pepper, finely diced

1. Combine all ingredients in the crockpot, mixing well.
2. Cover and cook on High for 1 hour.
3. Serve with baked tortilla chips or crudités.

CHAPTER 2

CHEESY SALSA DIP

Prep time: **10 minutes** | Cook time: **2 hours** | Serves **8**

- 225g reduced-fat soft cheese
- 100g grated reduced-fat mature Cheddar
- 45g mild or medium salsa
- 20ml semi-skimmed milk
- Tortilla chips or fresh vegetables to serve

1. Cut soft cheese into cubes.
2. Combine soft cheese, Cheddar, salsa and milk in the crockpot.
3. Cook on Low for 2 hours, stirring occasionally until smooth.
4. Serve hot with tortilla chips or fresh vegetables.

PICKLED WHITE FISH

Prep time: **10 minutes** | Cook time: **3-4 hours** | Serves **24**

- 2 onions, thinly sliced
- 100ml white wine vinegar
- 65g granulated sweetener
- 1 tsp salt
- 1 tbsp allspice
- 900g frozen whiting fillets (or other white fish), skin on

1. Combine onions, vinegar, sweetener, salt and allspice in crockpot.
2. Cut frozen fish into 5cm pieces, keeping skin on. Place in crockpot, ensuring fish is mostly covered by liquid.
3. Cook on Low for 3-4 hours.
4. Pour cooking liquid over fish, cover and refrigerate until thoroughly chilled before serving.

SWEET AND TANGY COCKTAIL SAUSAGES

Prep time: **10 minutes** | Cook time: **1-2 hours** | Serves **12**

- 340g redcurrant jelly
- 20g Dijon mustard
- 45ml dry sherry
- ¼ tsp ground allspice
- 435g tin pineapple chunks in juice
- 175g cocktail sausages

1. Melt jelly in crockpot on High. Stir in mustard, sherry and allspice until well combined.
2. Drain pineapple chunks, discarding juice. Add pineapple and sausages to crockpot.
3. Cover and cook on Low for 1-2 hours.
4. Serve hot as a party snack.

CREAMY POLENTA

Prep time: **5-10 minutes** | Cook time: **4-6 hours** | Serves **15-18**

- 200g polenta (cornmeal)
- 2 tsp salt
- 200ml cold water
- 600ml boiling water
- Butter, to serve

1. Mix polenta, salt and cold water.
2. Stir in boiling water. Pour into greased crockpot.
3. Cover and cook on High for 1 hour, then stir thoroughly and cook on Low for 3-4 hours. Alternatively, cook on Low for 5-6 hours, stirring hourly for the first 2 hours.
4. Serve hot with butter.

APPETIZERS AND SNACKS

BLUEBERRY BREAD AND BUTTER PUDDING

Prep time: 10-15 minutes | Cook time: 3-4 hours | Serves 12

- 1 large white bloomer or brioche loaf, cubed
- 300g fresh blueberries
- 225g full-fat soft cheese, cubed
- 6 large eggs
- 145ml whole milk
- Maple syrup or blueberry compote, to serve

1. Layer half the bread cubes in the crockpot.
2. Scatter over half the blueberries.
3. Dot with half the soft cheese.
4. Repeat layers with remaining ingredients.
5. Whisk together eggs and milk, then pour evenly over the layers.
6. Cover and cook on Low until custard is set.
7. Serve warm with maple syrup or blueberry compote.

SPICED APPLE BUTTER

Prep time: 10 minutes | Cook time: 12-16 hours | Makes 3.4 litres

- 100ml apple juice or cider
- 2.8 litres unsweetened apple sauce
- 200-300g caster sugar (adjust to taste)
- 1 tsp cider vinegar
- 1 tsp ground cinnamon
- ½ tsp ground allspice

1. In a small pan, reduce apple juice by boiling until 45ml remains.
2. Combine all ingredients in the crockpot.
3. Cover and cook on High for 12-16 hours, until mixture has reduced by half.
4. Transfer to sterilised jars or freezer containers.

KETO-FRIENDLY GRANOLA

Prep time: 10 minutes | Cook time: 3 to 4 hours | Serves 16

- 50g coconut oil, melted
- 2 tsp vanilla extract
- 1 tsp maple flavouring
- 100g pecan nuts, roughly chopped
- 100g sunflower seeds
- 100g desiccated coconut, unsweetened
- 50g hazelnuts
- 50g flaked almonds
- 25g granulated erythritol
- ½ tsp ground cinnamon
- ¼ tsp ground nutmeg
- ¼ tsp salt

1. Lightly grease the crockpot bowl with 1 tbsp coconut oil.
2. In a large bowl, whisk together remaining coconut oil, vanilla and maple flavouring. Add nuts, seeds, coconut, erythritol, and spices. Toss until evenly coated.
3. Transfer mixture to the crockpot.
4. Cover and cook on Low for 3-4 hours, until crispy.
5. Spread on a baking tray lined with baking parchment to cool.
6. Store in an airtight container in the fridge for up to 2 weeks.

CHAPTER 2

STAR ANISE APPLE BUTTER

Prep time: **15 minutes** | Cook time: **14-18 hours** | Makes **2.8 litres**

- 2.8kg cooking apples (such as Bramley)
- 200ml apple cider
- 30g caster sugar
- 1 whole star anise (optional)
- 2 tbsp lemon juice
- 2 cinnamon sticks

1. Peel, core and roughly chop the apples. Combine with cider in the crockpot.
2. Cover and cook on Low for 10-12 hours.
3. Stir in sugar, star anise, lemon juice and cinnamon sticks.
4. Cover and cook on High for 2 hours. Stir well.
5. Remove lid and cook on High for 2-4 hours more, until thickened.
6. Pour into sterilised jars and seal.

CRUNCHY CEREAL SNACK MIX

Prep time: **10 minutes** | Cook time: **2 hours** | Serves **10-14**

- 800g mixed cereals (such as Shreddies, Wheat Biscuits, Rice Snaps)
- 600g mixture of: pretzels, crackers, cheese crackers, oat hoops, nuts, bagel chips, corn snacks
- 85g butter, melted
- 2 tbsp Worcestershire sauce
- 1 tsp mixed seasoning salt
- ½ tsp garlic powder
- ½ tsp onion salt
- ½ tsp onion powder

1. Combine cereals and snack mixture in the crockpot.
2. Mix melted butter with all seasonings. Pour over dry ingredients and toss until well coated.
3. Cover and cook on Low for 2 hours, stirring every 30 minutes.

SAVOURY PARTY MIX

Prep time: **10 minutes** | Cook time: **3 hours** | Makes **3 litres**

- 300g pretzel sticks
- 400g Wheat Biscuits cereal
- 400g plain oat hoops cereal
- 350g salted peanuts
- 20g butter, melted
- 1 tsp garlic powder
- 1 tsp celery salt
- ½ tsp mixed seasoning salt
- 2 tbsp freshly grated Parmesan

1. Combine pretzels, cereals and peanuts in a large bowl.
2. Melt butter and stir in garlic powder, celery salt, seasoning salt and Parmesan. Pour over the dry ingredients. Toss until evenly coated.
3. Transfer to crockpot. Cover and cook on Low for 2½ hours, stirring every 30 minutes.
4. Remove lid and cook for a final 30 minutes on Low.
5. Serve warm or at room temperature. Store in an airtight container.

RICH HOT CHOCOLATE

Prep time: **10 minutes** | Cook time: **4 hours** | Serves **18**

For the chocolate syrup:

- 100g cocoa powder
- 200g caster sugar
- 100ml hot water
- ½ tsp vanilla extract

To serve:

- 3 litres whole milk

1. In a saucepan, whisk together cocoa powder, sugar and hot water. Bring to the boil and cook for 2 minutes.
2. Remove from heat and stir in vanilla extract.
3. Choose your preferred method:
    - Either heat the milk in a large pan, stir in the syrup, then transfer to the crockpot
    - Or place cold milk in the crockpot, heat until warm, then stir in the syrup
4. Keep warm in the crockpot throughout your party

CHAPTER 3: BREAKFASTS AND BRUNCHES

CHAPTER 3

CROCKPOT PORRIDGE

Prep time: **10 minutes** | Cook time: **2½-3 hours** | Serves **4-6**

- 20ml vegetable oil
- 45g caster sugar
- 1 large egg, beaten
- 200g porridge oats (quick-cooking)
- 1½ tsp baking powder
- ½ tsp salt
- 65ml whole milk

1. Grease the crockpot bowl with the oil, coating bottom and sides.
2. Add all remaining ingredients and mix thoroughly.
3. Cook on Low for 2½-3 hours.

BREAKFAST FRUIT COMPOTE

Prep time: **5 minutes** | Cook time: **2-7 hours** | Serves **8-9**

- 350g dried apricots
- 350g dried prunes
- 300g tin mandarin oranges in light syrup
- 800g tin sliced peaches in light syrup
- 20g sultanas
- 10 glacé cherries

1. Combine all ingredients in the crockpot and mix well.
2. Cover and cook on Low for 6-7 hours, or on High for 2-3 hours.

TRADITIONAL BOSTON BROWN BREAD

Prep time: **10 minutes** | Cook time: **3 to 4 hours** | Serves **6 to 8**

- 65g rye flour
- 65g wholemeal flour
- 65g fine cornmeal (polenta)
- 1¾ tsp bicarbonate of soda
- ½ tsp baking powder
- 1 tsp salt
- 140ml buttermilk
- 45g black treacle (or molasses)
- 45g butter, melted and slightly cooled
- 65g raisins
- 200ml boiling water

1. Fold four 30cm × 20cm pieces of foil in half twice to make 15cm × 10cm rectangles. Grease one side of each. Grease the inside of 4 clean 400g tins.
2. In a large bowl, whisk together the flours, cornmeal, bicarbonate of soda, baking powder and salt.
3. In another bowl, whisk buttermilk, treacle and melted butter. Stir in raisins.
4. Combine wet and dry ingredients until no dry flour remains. Divide between prepared tins and smooth tops. Cover tightly with prepared foil, greased side down.
5. Line crockpot with baking parchment. Add 1cm boiling water (about 200ml). Place tins in crockpot.
6. Cover and cook on High for 3-4 hours until a skewer comes out clean.
7. Cool in tins on a wire rack for 20 minutes, then turn out and cool completely.

BREAKFASTS AND BRUNCHES

KETO BREAKFAST BOWL

Prep time: 10 minutes | Cook time: 8 hours | Serves 6

- 15g coconut oil
- 100ml coconut milk
- 100g desiccated coconut, unsweetened
- 50g pecans, chopped
- 50g flaked almonds
- 25g granulated erythritol
- 1 ripe avocado, diced
- 60g protein powder
- 1 tsp ground cinnamon
- ¼ tsp ground nutmeg
- 50g blueberries, to serve

1. Grease the crockpot bowl with coconut oil.
2. Combine all ingredients except blueberries in the crockpot.
3. Cover and cook on Low for 8 hours.
4. Stir well to achieve desired consistency.
5. Serve topped with fresh blueberries.

PUMPKIN AND PECAN PORRIDGE

Prep time: 10 minutes | Cook time: 8 hours | Serves 4

- 1 tbsp coconut oil
- 300g butternut squash or pumpkin, cut into 2.5cm chunks
- 200ml coconut milk
- 50g ground pecans
- 30g plain protein powder
- 2 tbsp granulated erythritol
- 1 tsp maple flavouring
- ½ tsp ground nutmeg
- ¼ tsp ground cinnamon
- Pinch ground allspice

1. Grease the crockpot bowl with coconut oil.
2. Combine all remaining ingredients in the crockpot.
3. Cover and cook on Low for 8 hours.
4. Mash to desired consistency and serve.

TROPICAL BAKED PORRIDGE

Prep time: 5 minutes | Cook time: 1½-2½ hours | Serves 5-6

- 8 sachets instant porridge oats (about 320g total)
- 1½ tsp baking powder
- 2 eggs, beaten
- 45ml whole milk
- 220g tin crushed pineapple in juice

1. Lightly grease the crockpot bowl with cooking spray.
2. Empty porridge sachets into a large bowl and stir in baking powder.
3. Add eggs, milk and undrained pineapple. Mix thoroughly.
4. Pour into crockpot. Cover and cook on High for 1½ hours or Low for 2½ hours.

CINNAMON STREUSEL CAKE

Prep time: 10 minutes | Cook time: 3-4 hours | Serves 8-10

For the cake:
- 450g madeira cake mix, prepared as per packet instructions

For the streusel topping:
- 20g soft light brown sugar
- 1 tbsp plain flour
- 20g chopped nuts
- 1 tsp ground cinnamon

1. Thoroughly grease and flour a 900g loaf tin that fits in your crockpot. Pour in prepared cake mixture.
2. Mix brown sugar, flour, nuts and cinnamon. Sprinkle over cake batter.
3. Place tin in crockpot. Cover top of tin with several layers of kitchen paper.
4. Cover and cook on High for 3-4 hours until a skewer comes out clean.
5. Cool in tin for 30 minutes before serving.

CHAPTER 3

PULLED BBQ BEEF ROLLS

Prep time: **15 minutes** | Cook time: **8 hours** | Serves **8**

- 750g diced pork shoulder
- 500g braising steak, diced
- 170g tomato purée
- 20ml cider vinegar
- 45g soft dark brown sugar
- 1 tsp salt
- 1 tbsp mild chilli powder
- 1 large onion, chopped
- 1 green pepper, chopped
- Soft bread rolls, to serve
- Coleslaw, to serve

1. Combine all ingredients except rolls and coleslaw in the crockpot.
2. Cover and cook on Low for 8 hours.
3. Shred meat using two forks.
4. Serve in soft rolls with creamy coleslaw.

CHEESY POLENTA WITH GREEN CHILLIES

Prep time: **10 minutes** | Cook time: **2-6 hours** | Serves **10-12**

- 50g quick-cook polenta
- 400g processed cheese, cubed
- ½ tsp garlic powder
- 2 × 110g tins green chillies, diced
- 100g butter

1. Prepare polenta according to packet instructions.
2. Stir in cheese, garlic powder and chillies until cheese melts.
3. Add butter and stir until melted. Transfer to greased crockpot.
4. Cover and cook on High for 2-3 hours or Low for 4-6 hours.

SAUSAGE AND CHEESE BREAKFAST STRATA

Prep time: **10 minutes** | Cook time: **3 to 4 hours** | Serves **4**

- 225g pork sausagemeat
- 1 onion, finely chopped
- 1 tbsp vegetable oil
- 2 garlic cloves, finely chopped
- 2 tsp fresh thyme leaves or ½ tsp dried
- 1.2kg day-old crusty white bread, cut into 1cm cubes
- 170g mature Cheddar, grated
- 50ml single cream
- 9 large eggs
- Salt and freshly ground black pepper
- 2 tbsp fresh chives, finely chopped

1. Line crockpot with foil collar, then press 2 large sheets of foil perpendicular to each other, with excess hanging over edges. Lightly grease with oil.
2. Microwave sausagemeat, onion, oil, garlic and thyme, stirring and breaking up meat occasionally, until sausage is cooked through (6-8 minutes).
3. Layer half the bread in prepared crockpot, top with half the sausage mixture and 45g cheese. Repeat layers with remaining bread, sausage and 100g cheese.
4. Whisk cream, eggs, 1 tsp salt and ½ tsp pepper. Pour evenly over bread, pressing gently to submerge.
5. Cover and cook on Low for 3-4 hours until set.
6. Stand covered for 20 minutes before serving scattered with chives.

BREAKFASTS AND BRUNCHES

SIMPLE HOMINY PORRIDGE

Prep time: **5 minutes** | Cook time: **8 hours** | Serves **5**

- 100g dried hominy (corn grits)
- 1 tsp salt
- Freshly ground black pepper (optional)
- 300ml water
- 30g butter

1. Combine all ingredients in a greased crockpot.
2. Cover and cook on Low for 8 hours or overnight.
3. Serve warm for breakfast.

SPICED PEAR PORRIDGE

Prep time: **5 minutes** | Cook time: **8 hours** | Serves **4**

- 65g steel-cut oats
- ⅛ tsp ground cardamom
- ⅛ tsp ground nutmeg
- ⅛ tsp ground ginger
- ¼ tsp ground cinnamon
- ⅛ tsp sea salt
- 1 ripe pear, peeled, cored and diced
- 300ml unsweetened almond milk or water

1. Combine oats and spices in the crockpot.
2. Add pear and almond milk, stirring well.
3. Cover and cook on Low for 8 hours or overnight.

LEEK, BACON AND GOAT'S CHEESE STRATA

Prep time: **10 minutes** | Cook time: **3 to 4 hours** | Serves **4**

- 450g leeks, white and light green parts only, halved, sliced and well washed
- 10 rashers streaky bacon, finely chopped
- 2 garlic cloves, finely chopped
- 2 tsp fresh thyme leaves or ½ tsp dried
- 1.2kg day-old crusty bread, cut into 1cm pieces
- 170g soft goat's cheese, crumbled
- 50ml single cream
- 9 large eggs
- Salt and freshly ground black pepper
- 2 tbsp fresh chives, finely chopped

1. Line crockpot with foil collar, then two sheets of foil perpendicular to each other, with excess hanging over edges. Lightly oil.
2. Microwave leeks, bacon, garlic and thyme, stirring occasionally, until leeks soften (8-10 minutes).
3. Layer half the bread in crockpot, top with half the leek mixture and 65g cheese. Repeat layers.
4. Whisk cream, eggs, 1 tsp salt and ½ tsp pepper. Pour over bread, pressing gently to submerge.
5. Cover and cook on Low for 3-4 hours until set.
6. Stand covered for 20 minutes, then scatter with chives and serve.

CHAPTER 3

SPICED BREAKFAST PRUNES

Prep time: **10 minutes** | Cook time: **8-10 hours** | Serves **6**

- 200ml orange juice
- 20g orange marmalade
- 1 tsp ground cinnamon
- ¼ tsp ground cloves
- ¼ tsp ground nutmeg
- 100ml water
- 350g ready-to-eat dried prunes
- 2 thin lemon slices

1. Combine juice, marmalade, spices and water in crockpot.
2. Add prunes and lemon slices.
3. Cover and cook on Low for 8-10 hours or overnight.
4. Serve warm for breakfast or as a accompaniment any time.

APPLE AND BLUEBERRY COMPOTE

Prep time: **10 minutes** | Cook time: **3 hours** | Serves **10-12**

- 1 litre unsweetened apple sauce
- 2 Bramley apples, unpeeled, cored and sliced
- 300g fresh or frozen blueberries
- ½ tbsp ground cinnamon
- 45ml pure maple syrup
- 1 tsp almond extract
- 45g walnuts, roughly chopped

1. Coat crockpot with cooking spray. Combine apple sauce, apples and blueberries.
2. Add cinnamon and maple syrup.
3. Cover and cook on Low for 3 hours.
4. Stir in almond extract and walnuts before serving.

MEDITERRANEAN VEGETABLE HASH WITH EGGS

Prep time: **20 minutes** | Cook time: **6¼ hours** | Serves **2**

- Cooking spray
- 1 onion, chopped
- 2 garlic cloves, finely chopped
- 1 red pepper, chopped
- 1 courgette, chopped
- 2 carrots, chopped
- 2 Maris Piper potatoes, peeled and chopped
- 2 large tomatoes, deseeded and chopped
- 20ml vegetable stock
- ½ tsp salt
- ⅛ tsp freshly ground black pepper
- ½ tsp dried thyme
- 3-4 large eggs
- ½ tsp sweet paprika

1. Lightly coat crockpot with cooking spray.
2. Combine all ingredients except eggs and paprika in the crockpot.
3. Cover and cook on Low for 6 hours.
4. Make an indentation for each egg. Break eggs into cup first, then slip into indentations.
5. Sprinkle with paprika.
6. Cover and cook on Low for 10-15 minutes until eggs are just set.

BREAKFASTS AND BRUNCHES

TRADITIONAL PORRIDGE

Prep time: 5 minutes | Cook time: 8 hours | Serves 6

- 200g porridge oats
- 400ml water
- 1 tsp salt
- 145g chopped dates, raisins or dried cranberries (or a mixture)

1. Combine all ingredients in crockpot.
   - Cover and cook on Low overnight, or for 8 hours.

CHERRY AND QUINOA PORRIDGE

Prep time: 5 minutes | Cook time: 8 hours | Serves 4

- 65g quinoa
- 50g dried cherries
- ⅛ tsp sea salt
- 1 tsp vanilla extract
- 300ml almond milk or water

1. Combine quinoa, cherries and salt in crockpot.
2. Add vanilla and almond milk, stirring well.
3. Cover and cook on Low for 8 hours or overnight.

BEETROOT HASH WITH POACHED EGGS

Prep time: 10 minutes | Cook time: 5 to 6 hours | Serves 6

- 1 onion, finely chopped
- 2 garlic cloves, finely chopped
- 1 tbsp vegetable oil
- 2 tsp fresh thyme leaves or ½ tsp dried
- 1 tsp paprika
- Salt and freshly ground black pepper
- 900g Maris Piper potatoes, peeled and diced
- 350g raw beetroot, peeled and diced
- 45ml vegetable or chicken stock
- 20ml double cream
- 6 large eggs
- 2 spring onions, finely sliced
- Hot sauce, to serve

1. Line crockpot with foil collar and lightly oil. Microwave onion, garlic, oil, thyme, paprika and 1 tsp salt until onion softens (about 3 minutes).
2. Add potatoes and beetroot, toss to combine and transfer to crockpot. Pour over stock.
3. Cover and cook until vegetables are tender (5-6 hours on Low or 3-4 hours on High).
4. Remove foil collar. Mash 200g of vegetables with cream until smooth. Fold back into crockpot and smooth surface.
5. Make 6 wells in the hash. Crack an egg into each, season with salt and pepper.
6. Cover and cook on High for 20-30 minutes until egg whites are just setting.
7. Turn off and leave covered for 5 minutes.
8. Garnish with spring onions and serve with hot sauce.

CHAPTER 3

SPICED SWEET POTATO HASH

Prep time: **10 minutes** | Cook time: **8 hours** | Serves **4**

- 15g butter, softened, or olive oil
- 4 large eggs
- 50ml semi-skimmed milk
- ⅛ tsp sea salt
- ½ tsp smoked paprika
- ½ tsp ground cumin
- Freshly ground black pepper
- 100g sweet potato, finely diced
- 100g frozen sweetcorn, thawed
- 50g roasted red peppers, diced
- 2 tbsp onion, finely chopped

1. Grease crockpot with butter.
2. Whisk eggs, milk, salt, paprika and cumin. Season with black pepper.
3. Add sweet potato, sweetcorn, peppers and onion to crockpot.
4. Pour in egg mixture and stir gently.
5. Cover and cook on Low for 8 hours or overnight.

FESTIVE MORNING PUNCH

Prep time: **5-10 minutes** | Cook time: **3 hours** | Makes **4 quarts**

- 2 litres cranberry juice
- 1 litre apple juice
- 340ml frozen pineapple juice concentrate
- 340ml frozen lemonade concentrate
- 3-4 cinnamon sticks
- 1 litre water (optional)

1. Combine all ingredients except water in crockpot.
2. Add water if mixture is too sweet.
3. Cover and cook on Low for 3 hours.
4. Serve hot in mugs.

COURGETTE AND MUSHROOM BREAKFAST BAKE

Prep time: **20 minutes** | Cook time: **6 hours** | Serves **2**

- 1 onion, chopped
- 2 garlic cloves, finely chopped
- 85g chestnut mushrooms, sliced
- 1 red pepper, chopped
- 1 courgette, chopped
- Cooking spray
- 6 slices crusty white bread, cubed
- 100g mature Cheddar, grated
- 100g Gruyère cheese, grated
- 5 large eggs, beaten
- 100ml whole milk
- 1 tbsp Dijon mustard
- ½ tsp salt
- ½ tsp dried basil
- ⅛ tsp freshly ground black pepper

1. Combine onion, garlic, mushrooms, pepper and courgette in a bowl.
2. Lightly coat crockpot with cooking spray.
3. Layer bread, vegetable mixture and cheeses in the crockpot.
4. Whisk together eggs, milk, mustard, salt, basil and pepper.
5. Pour egg mixture into crockpot.
6. Cover and cook on Low for 6 hours, or until centre reaches 70°C.
7. Cut into squares to serve.

CHAPTER 4: POULTRY

CHAPTER 4

GREEK-STYLE CHICKEN PITTA FILLING

Prep time: **10 minutes** | Cook time: **6-8 hours** | Serves **4**

- 1 onion, chopped
- 450g boneless, skinless chicken thighs
- 1 tsp lemon pepper seasoning
- ½ tsp dried oregano
- 45g Greek-style natural yoghurt

1. Put onion and chicken in crockpot, sprinkle with lemon pepper.
2. Cover and cook on Low for 6-8 hours until chicken is tender.
3. Remove chicken and shred using two forks.
4. Return to crockpot, stir in oregano and yoghurt.
5. Serve in warm pitta breads.

MEXICAN GREEN CHILLI CHICKEN WRAPS

Prep time: **10 minutes** | Cook time: **4 to 5 hours** | Serves **4 to 6**

- 100g green chilli salsa
- 2 green chillies, deseeded and chopped
- Salt and freshly ground black pepper
- 1 tsp fresh oregano or ¼ tsp dried
- 1.4kg boneless, skinless chicken thighs, trimmed
- 20g fresh basil, finely chopped
- 2 tbsp lime juice
- 12-18 soft flour tortillas, warmed

1. Combine salsa, chillies, ¼ tsp each salt and pepper, and oregano in crockpot.
2. Season chicken with salt and pepper, add to crockpot.
3. Cover and cook on Low for 4-5 hours until tender.
4. Shred chicken using tongs. Stir in basil and lime juice.
5. Season to taste and serve in warm tortillas.

GARLIC BRAISED CHICKEN THIGHS

Prep time: **15 minutes** | Cook time: **7 to 8 hours** | Serves **4**

- 25ml extra virgin olive oil, divided
- 700g boneless chicken thighs
- 1 tsp paprika
- Salt and freshly ground black pepper
- 1 large onion, chopped
- 4 garlic cloves, thinly sliced
- 50ml chicken stock
- 2 tbsp fresh lemon juice
- 50g Greek-style yoghurt

1. Lightly oil crockpot with 1 tbsp olive oil.
2. Season chicken with paprika, salt and pepper.
3. Heat remaining oil in large frying pan. Brown chicken for 5 minutes, turning once.
4. Transfer to crockpot. Add onion, garlic, stock and lemon juice.
5. Cover and cook on Low for 7-8 hours.
6. Stir in yoghurt before serving.

JAPANESE TERIYAKI CHICKEN

Prep time: **10 minutes** | Cook time: **2 hours** | Serves **4**

- 4 skinless chicken breasts or 6 skinless chicken thighs
- 60ml sake (or dry white wine)
- 2 tbsp mirin (sweet rice wine)
- 4 tsp soy sauce
- 1 tsp soft light brown sugar

1. Heat a heavy-based frying pan until very hot. Brown chicken smooth side down (2-4 minutes), then turn.
2. Transfer to crockpot, smooth side up.
3. Add sake, mirin, soy sauce and sugar to pan. Scrape up browned bits.
4. Pour sauce over chicken. Cover and cook on High for 2 hours (breasts) or 3 hours (thighs).

POULTRY

CREAMY MUSHROOM CHICKEN

Prep time: 10-15 minutes | Cook time: 4-5 hours | Serves 4

- 4 skinless chicken breasts
- 295g tin cream of mushroom soup
- 240ml soured cream
- 200g tin mushrooms, drained (optional)
- 4 rashers streaky bacon, cooked and crumbled
- Cooked rice or pasta, to serve

1. Place chicken in crockpot.
2. Mix soup, soured cream and mushrooms (if using). Pour over chicken.
3. Cover and cook on Low for 4-5 hours until chicken is tender but not dry.
4. Sprinkle with crumbled bacon before serving.
5. Serve over rice or pasta.

SPICY CHICKEN LETTUCE WRAPS

Prep time: 15 minutes | Cook time: 10 hours | Serves 8

- 4 skinless chicken breasts
- 240ml tomato salsa
- 1 tsp onion powder
- 1 tin green chillies, chopped
- 15ml hot pepper sauce
- 30ml fresh lime juice
- Salt and freshly ground black pepper
- 2 large iceberg lettuces
- Soured cream, diced tomatoes and sliced avocado, to serve

1. Place chicken in crockpot.
2. Add salsa, onion powder, chillies, hot sauce and lime juice. Season well.
3. Cover and cook on Low for 10 hours.
4. Shred chicken using two forks.
5. Serve wrapped in lettuce leaves with optional toppings.

CHICKEN IN RICH BACON GRAVY

Prep time: 35 minutes | Cook time: 7 hours | Serves 4

- 680g skinless, boneless chicken breasts
- ¼ tsp freshly ground black pepper
- 1 tsp salt
- 1 tsp garlic, finely chopped
- 1 tsp dried thyme
- 6 rashers streaky bacon, cooked and crumbled
- 350ml water
- 150ml double cream

1. Combine all ingredients except cream in crockpot.
2. Cook on Low for 6 hours.
3. Stir in cream and cook for a further hour.

ITALIAN-STYLE CHICKEN SAUSAGES WITH BEANS

Prep time: 10 minutes | Cook time: 3 to 4 hours | Serves 4

- 2 × 400g tins cannellini beans, drained and rinsed
- 20ml chicken stock
- 20ml dry white wine
- 2 garlic cloves, finely chopped
- 1 fresh rosemary sprig
- Salt and freshly ground black pepper
- 700g Italian-style chicken sausages
- 250g cherry tomatoes
- 400g baby spinach
- 2 tbsp extra virgin olive oil

1. Combine beans, stock, wine, garlic, rosemary, ½ tsp salt and ½ tsp pepper in crockpot.
2. Add sausages and top with tomatoes.
3. Cover and cook on Low for 3-4 hours until sausages are tender.
4. Transfer sausages to serving dish and cover with foil.
5. Remove rosemary. Mash 100g of bean mixture until smooth.
6. Stir in spinach and mashed beans. Leave for 5 minutes until spinach wilts.
7. Stir in oil and season to taste. Serve sausages with bean ragout.

CHAPTER 4

MEDITERRANEAN CHICKEN WITH TOMATOES AND OLIVES

Prep time: 5 minutes | **Cook time:** 7 hours | Serves 4

- 240ml water
- 400g chicken drumsticks
- 1 tbsp fresh thyme leaves
- 200g cherry tomatoes, halved
- 200g black olives, pitted and halved
- 1 tsp salt
- 1 tsp paprika
- 1 tbsp olive oil
- ½ tsp black peppercorns

1. In the crockpot, mix the chicken with thyme, tomatoes and the other ingredients.
   - Close the crockpot lid and cook the mix for 7 hours on Low.

POUSSIN WITH ROOT VEGETABLES

Prep time: 15 minutes | **Cook time:** 8 hours on low | Serves 2

- 2 poussins (young chickens)
- ½ tsp salt
- ½ tsp poultry seasoning
- ⅛ tsp freshly ground black pepper
- 1 small lemon, cut into 8 wedges
- 100g chestnut mushrooms, sliced
- 2 carrots, sliced
- 1 onion, chopped
- 2 garlic cloves, finely chopped
- 2 Maris Piper potatoes, diced
- 45ml chicken stock

1. Season poussins with salt, poultry seasoning and pepper. Place lemon wedges in cavities.
2. Layer mushrooms, carrots, onion, garlic and potatoes in crockpot.
3. Place poussins on vegetables and pour over stock.
4. Cover and cook on Low for 8 hours until poussins reach 74°C.
5. Serve poussins with vegetables.

CHICKEN AND PRAWN RICE

Prep time: 15-20 minutes | **Cook time:** 3-8 hours | Serves 4-6

- 120g long-grain rice
- 45g butter, melted
- 300ml chicken stock
- 350g cooked chicken breast, diced
- 2 × 110g tins sliced mushrooms, drained
- 20ml soy sauce
- 350g frozen prawns, defrosted
- 8 spring onions, chopped (reserve 2 tbsp)
- 55g flaked almonds

1. Combine rice and butter in crockpot, coating rice well.
2. Add remaining ingredients except almonds and reserved spring onions.
3. Cover and cook on Low for 6-8 hours or High for 3-4 hours until rice is tender.
4. Garnish with almonds and reserved spring onions.

QUICK CHICKEN SOUP

Prep time: 20 minutes | **Cook time:** 3¼-4¼ hours | Serves 3-4

- Leftover cooked chicken and stock
- 2 carrots, thinly sliced
- 1 celery stick, sliced
- 2 medium onions, roughly chopped
- 2 tbsp plain flour or cornflour
- 20ml cold water
- Cooked rice or pasta, to serve

1. Remove chicken from bones and set aside.
2. Return stock to crockpot. Add carrots, celery and onions.
3. Cook on High for 3-4 hours.
4. Mix flour with cold water until smooth. Stir into hot stock.
5. Add chicken and cook for 15-20 minutes until thickened and chicken is hot.
6. Serve over rice or pasta.

POULTRY

BACON AND FETA-STUFFED CHICKEN

Prep time: **10 minutes** | Cook time: **1½-3 hours** | Serves **4**

- 20g cooked bacon, crumbled
- 20g feta cheese, crumbled
- 4 skinless chicken breasts
- 400g tin chopped tomatoes
- 1 tbsp dried basil

1. Mix bacon and feta together.
2. Cut a pocket in each chicken breast. Fill with bacon mixture.
3. Secure with cocktail sticks.
4. Place in crockpot. Top with tomatoes and basil.
5. Cover and cook on High for 1½-3 hours until chicken is cooked but still moist.

CHICKEN AND SAGE STUFFING BAKE

Prep time: **10 minutes** | Cook time: **2-3 hours** | Serves **4-6**

- 400g cooked chicken
- 1 packet sage and onion stuffing mix
- 2 large eggs
- 100ml water
- 100ml milk
- 100g frozen peas

1. Mix chicken with dry stuffing mix in crockpot.
2. Whisk eggs, water and milk. Pour over chicken mixture.
3. Cover and cook on High for 2-3 hours.
4. Add peas for final hour of cooking.

ITALIAN-STYLE BRAISED TURKEY SAUSAGES

Prep time: **10 minutes** | Cook time: **3 to 4 hours** | Serves **4**

- 350g new potatoes, unpeeled, quartered and sliced 5mm thick
- 3 mixed peppers (red, yellow or green), deseeded and cut into 5mm strips
- 1 onion, halved and sliced
- 20g tomato purée
- 2 tablespoons water
- 3 garlic cloves, finely chopped
- 2 teaspoons fresh oregano, chopped (or ½ teaspoon dried)
- ¼ teaspoon dried chilli flakes
- 20ml chicken stock
- 680g Italian-style turkey sausages
- 2 tablespoons fresh basil, chopped
- Salt and freshly ground black pepper

1. Place potatoes, peppers, onion, tomato purée, water, garlic, oregano and chilli flakes in a microwaveable bowl. Cover and microwave, stirring occasionally, until vegetables are nearly tender (about 15 minutes). Transfer to the crockpot and stir in the stock.
2. Nestle the sausages into the vegetable mixture.
3. Cover and cook on Low for 3-4 hours, until sausages and vegetables are tender.
4. Transfer sausages to a serving dish. Stir basil into the vegetable mixture and season with salt and pepper to taste. Spoon vegetables over sausages and serve.

CHAPTER 4

SPICY CHICKEN WITH RICE

Prep time: **10 minutes** | Cook time: **4-6 hours** | Serves **4**

- 100g long-grain rice, uncooked
- 120ml chicken stock
- 100g tomato salsa (mild, medium or hot)
- 4 skinless chicken breast fillets
- 65g mature Cheddar, grated

1. Lightly grease the inside of the crockpot with cooking oil.
2. Add the rice to the crockpot.
3. Pour in the chicken stock and salsa. Stir to combine.
4. Lay the chicken breasts on top.
5. Cover and cook on Low for 4-6 hours, until both chicken and rice are tender but not dry.
6. Sprinkle with grated cheese just before serving.

CHICKEN, BROCCOLI AND RICE BAKE

Prep time: **10 minutes** | Cook time: **3-7 hours** | Serves **8**

- 100g long-grain rice, uncooked
- 300ml water
- 2 chicken stock cubes, crumbled
- 1 tin (295g) condensed cream of chicken soup
- 200g cooked chicken breast, chopped
- ¼ teaspoon garlic powder
- 1 teaspoon onion salt
- 100g reduced-fat Cheddar, grated
- 450g frozen broccoli florets, thawed

1. Combine all ingredients except broccoli in the crockpot.
2. One hour before the end of cooking time, stir in the broccoli.
3. Cook on High for 3-4 hours total, or on Low for 6-7 hours.

MEDITERRANEAN CHICKEN ROLLS

Prep time: **15 minutes** | Cook time: **7 hours** | Serves **2**

- 1 onion, sliced
- 2 garlic cloves, sliced
- 1 carrot, julienned
- 1 red pepper, chopped
- 5 boneless, skinless chicken thighs
- ½ tsp salt
- ½ tsp dried thyme
- ⅛ tsp freshly ground black pepper
- 20ml chicken stock
- 2 crusty rolls, split and toasted
- 2 tbsp mayonnaise
- 2 tbsp wholegrain mustard

1. Layer onion, garlic, carrot and pepper in crockpot.
2. Season chicken with salt, thyme and pepper. Place on vegetables.
3. Pour over stock. Cover and cook on Low for 7 hours until chicken reaches 74°C.
4. Shred chicken and return to crockpot. Stir well.
5. Spread rolls with mayonnaise and mustard. Fill with chicken mixture.

POULTRY

CHICKEN WITH MUSHROOMS AND SHALLOTS

Prep time: 10 minutes | Cook time: 6 to 8 hours | Serves 4

- 1 teaspoon unsalted butter, softened, or extra virgin olive oil
- 200g chestnut mushrooms, thinly sliced
- 1 teaspoon fresh thyme leaves
- 2 garlic cloves, finely chopped
- 1 banana shallot, finely chopped
- 3 tablespoons dry sherry
- 2 chicken thighs (bone in, skin removed), about 170g each
- ⅛ teaspoon sea salt
- Freshly ground black pepper

1. Grease the inside of the crockpot with the butter or oil.
2. Add the mushrooms, thyme, garlic and shallot to the crockpot, tossing gently to combine. Pour in the sherry.
3. Season the chicken with salt and pepper and place on top of the mushroom mixture.
4. Cover and cook on Low for 6-8 hours.

ASIAN CHICKEN GINGER

Prep time: 15 minutes | Cook time: 4-6 hours | Serves 6

- 6 chicken breast fillets, cut into chunks
- 100g carrots, diced
- 45g onion, finely chopped
- 45ml light soy sauce
- 20ml rice wine vinegar
- 20g sesame seeds
- 1 tablespoon ground ginger (or 20g fresh root ginger, grated)
- ¾ teaspoon salt
- 1 teaspoon sesame oil
- 200g broccoli florets
- 100g cauliflower florets

1. Combine all ingredients except broccoli and cauliflower in the crockpot.
2. Cover and cook on Low for 3-5 hours. Add broccoli and cauliflower and cook for an additional hour.
3. Serve over brown rice.

ITALIAN CHICKEN STEW

Prep time: 20 minutes | Cook time: 3-6 hours | Serves 4

- 2 skinless chicken breast fillets, cut into 4cm pieces
- 1 tin (400g) cannellini beans, drained and rinsed
- 1 tin (400g) kidney beans, drained and rinsed
- 1 tin (400g) chopped tomatoes
- 100g celery, chopped
- 100g carrots, sliced
- 2 small garlic cloves, roughly chopped
- 100ml water
- 45ml red wine (or chicken stock)
- 3 tablespoons tomato purée
- 1 tablespoon caster sugar
- 1½ teaspoons dried Italian herbs

1. Place chicken, both types of beans, tomatoes, celery, carrots and garlic in the crockpot. Mix well.
2. In a medium bowl, combine all remaining ingredients. Mix well and pour over the chicken and vegetables. Stir to combine.
3. Cover and cook on Low for 5-6 hours, or on High for 3 hours.

CHAPTER 5:
RED MEATS

RED MEATS

FRUITED PORK

Prep time: **10 minutes** | Cook time: **4-6 hours** | Serves **6**

- 900g boneless pork loin joint
- ½ teaspoon salt
- ¼ teaspoon freshly ground black pepper
- 120g mixed dried fruit
- 45ml apple juice

1. Place pork in crockpot and season with salt and pepper.
2. Scatter dried fruit over the top and pour over the apple juice.
3. Cover and cook on Low for 4-6 hours, until pork is tender.

APPLE AND CRANBERRY PORK

Prep time: **20 minutes** | Cook time: **6-8 hours** | Serves **8**

- 900g pork tenderloin, trimmed
- 2 tablespoons vegetable oil
- 300ml apple juice
- 3 Bramley apples, peeled and sliced
- 100g fresh cranberries
- ¾ teaspoon salt
- ½ teaspoon freshly ground black pepper

1. Heat oil in a frying pan and brown the pork on all sides. Transfer to crockpot.
2. Add remaining ingredients.
3. Cover and cook on Low for 6-8 hours.

ITALIAN-STYLE ROAST WITH POTATOES

Prep time: **30-35 minutes** | Cook time: **6-7 hours** | Serves **8**

- 6 medium potatoes, peeled (optional) and quartered
- 1 large onion, sliced
- 1.4-1.8kg boneless beef joint
- 700g jar Italian pasta sauce with basil
- 45ml water
- 3 beef stock cubes

1. Layer potatoes and onion in the bottom of the crockpot.
2. Meanwhile, brown the joint on all sides in a non-stick frying pan.
3. Place joint on top of vegetables. Pour over any meat juices from the pan.
4. Mix 100g pasta sauce with 45ml water in a small bowl. Crumble in stock cubes and stir well. Spoon over the meat.
5. Cover and cook on Low for 6-7 hours, until meat is tender but not dry.
6. Transfer joint and vegetables to a serving platter. Cover with foil to keep warm.
7. Pour 100g of cooking liquor from the crockpot into a medium saucepan. Stir in remaining pasta sauce and heat through.
8. Carve the beef and serve with the heated sauce.

CHAPTER 5

GINGER BEEF

Prep time: **15 minutes** | Cook time: **9 to 10 hours** | Serves **8**

- 25ml extra virgin olive oil, divided
- 900g beef chuck, rolled
- ½ teaspoon salt
- 50ml beef stock
- 25g sugar-free ketchup
- 2 tablespoons cider vinegar
- 2 tablespoons fresh root ginger, grated

1. Lightly grease the crockpot with 1 tablespoon of olive oil.
2. Heat remaining oil in a large frying pan over medium-high heat.
3. Season beef with salt and brown for 6 minutes. Transfer to crockpot.
4. Combine stock, ketchup, vinegar and ginger in a small bowl. Pour over the beef.
5. Cover and cook on Low for 9-10 hours.
6. Serve hot.

BALSAMIC BEEF WITH RED CABBAGE

Prep time: **5 minutes** | Cook time: **8 hours** | Serves **4**

- 350g braising steak, trimmed and cut into 2.5cm chunks
- 200g red cabbage, shredded
- 50g red onion, thinly sliced
- 25ml dry red wine
- 5ml balsamic vinegar
- 1 teaspoon Dijon mustard
- 1 teaspoon ground cumin
- ⅛ teaspoon sea salt
- Freshly ground black pepper

1. Place beef in the crockpot, top with cabbage and onions.
2. Whisk together wine, vinegar, mustard, cumin, salt and a few grinds of black pepper in a small bowl. Pour over the ingredients in the crockpot.
3. Cover and cook on Low for 8 hours.

EMERGENCY FROZEN ROAST BEEF

Prep time: **20 minutes** | Cook time: **7-9 hours** | Serves **10**

- 1.4-1.8kg frozen beef joint
- 1½ teaspoons salt
- Freshly ground black pepper
- 1 large onion
- 20g plain flour
- 65ml cold water

1. Place frozen joint in the crockpot. Season with salt and pepper. Slice onion and arrange over the top.
2. Cover and cook on High for 1 hour. Reduce to Low and cook for 6-8 hours, until meat is tender but not dry.
3. For the gravy, transfer 120ml of cooking liquor from the crockpot into a saucepan. Bring to the boil.
4. Meanwhile, mix flour and cold water in a small bowl until smooth.
5. Gradually whisk the flour mixture into the boiling liquor, stirring constantly until smooth and thickened.
6. Slice the joint and return meat and onions to the crockpot. Pour gravy over. Keep warm on Low until ready to serve.

RED MEATS

TRADITIONAL PORK AND SAUERKRAUT

Prep time: 30 minutes | Cook time: 10-11 hours | Serves 10-15

- 1.8-2.3kg lean pork loin joint
- 450-900g sauerkraut, divided
- ½ small white cabbage, finely sliced, divided
- 1 large onion, finely sliced, divided
- 1 cooking apple, quartered, cored and sliced (skin on), divided
- 1 teaspoon dried dill (optional)
- 45g soft brown sugar (optional)
- 100ml water

1. Brown the joint for 10 minutes in a heavy non-stick frying pan. Transfer to the crockpot.
2. Layer with half the sauerkraut, followed by half the cabbage, half the onion, and half the apple.
3. Repeat the layers with remaining ingredients.
4. If using, mix dill, brown sugar and water in a bowl and pour over. Otherwise, just add the water.
5. Cover and cook on High for 1 hour. Reduce to Low and cook for 9-10 hours, until meat is tender.

AUTUMN HARVEST PORK LOIN

Prep time: 30 minutes | Cook time: 5-6 hours | Serves 4-6

- 100ml dry cider or apple juice
- 700-900g pork loin joint
- Salt and freshly ground black pepper
- 2 large Bramley apples, peeled and sliced
- 1½ butternut squash, peeled and cubed
- 45g soft brown sugar
- ¼ teaspoon ground cinnamon
- ¼ teaspoon dried thyme
- ¼ teaspoon dried sage

1. Heat cider in a large frying pan. Sear pork loin on all sides in the cider.
2. Season meat with salt and pepper. Place in crockpot with cooking juices.
3. Mix apples and squash. Sprinkle with sugar and herbs, stir, then arrange around pork.
4. Cover and cook on Low for 5-6 hours.
5. Remove pork and rest for 10-15 minutes. Carve into 1cm-thick slices.
6. Serve topped with the apple and squash mixture.

BEEF RIBS

Prep time: 5 minutes | Cook time: 8½ hours | Serves 8-10

- 1.4-1.8kg beef short ribs
- 150ml BBQ sauce, divided
- 45g apricot or pineapple jam
- 1 tablespoon light soy sauce

1. Place ribs in a roasting tin.
2. Mix 65ml BBQ sauce with jam and soy sauce. Pour over ribs. Roast at 230°C/Gas Mark 8 for 30 minutes to brown.
3. Transfer ribs and cooking juices to the crockpot.
4. Cover and cook on Low for 8 hours.
5. Mix remaining BBQ sauce with cooking juices and pour over ribs before serving.

PORK CHOPS IN TOMATO SAUCE

Prep time: 25 minutes | Cook time: 3-7 hours | Serves 4-6

- 4 thick-cut pork chops
- 1 medium onion, sliced
- 45g tomato ketchup
- 20g soft brown sugar
- ½ teaspoon chilli powder
- 45ml water

1. Arrange pork chops in the crockpot. Top with onions.
2. Mix ketchup, sugar, chilli powder and water in a bowl. Spoon sauce over chops. (If stacking chops, ensure each layer is sauced.)
3. Cover and cook on High for 3-4 hours, or on Low for 6-7 hours, until tender but not dry.

31

CHAPTER 5

TEX-MEX BEEF

Prep time: **5-10 minutes** | Cook time: **4-10 hours** | Serves **6**

- 1.4-1.8kg beef short ribs or braising steak, cut into serving portions
- 100ml steak sauce (such as HP)
- 20g hot salsa
- 1 teaspoon chilli powder
- ½ teaspoon English mustard powder

1. Place meat in crockpot.
2. Combine remaining ingredients in a bowl and pour over meat.
3. Cover and cook on Low for 4-10 hours, until meat is tender but not overcooked.

SWEET AND SAVORY BRISKET

Prep time: **10-12 minutes** | Cook time: **8-10 hours** | Serves **8-10**

- 1.4-1.6kg fresh beef brisket, cut in half
- 100g tomato ketchup
- 20g grape jelly (or redcurrant jelly)
- 1 packet dry onion soup mix
- ½ teaspoon freshly ground black pepper

1. Place half of the brisket in the crockpot.
2. Mix ketchup, jelly, soup mix and pepper in a bowl.
3. Spread half the mixture over the meat. Top with remaining brisket and remaining ketchup mixture.
4. Cover and cook on Low for 8-10 hours until meat is tender but not dry.
5. Rest meat for 10 minutes before carving. Serve with cooking juices.

SAUSAGE AND VEGETABLE CASSEROLE

Prep time: **30 minutes** | Cook time: **3-10 hours** | Serves **10**

- 450g good-quality sausages (pork, turkey, or smoked)
- 400g potatoes, cooked and diced
- 400g carrots, cooked and sliced
- 400g green beans, cooked
- 800g passata
- 1 teaspoon onion powder
- ¼-½ teaspoon freshly ground black pepper, to taste

1. Cut sausages into 4cm pieces. Place in crockpot.
2. Add cooked vegetables. Pour passata over.
3. Season with onion powder and pepper. Stir to combine.
4. Cook on High for 3-4 hours, or on Low for 8-10 hours.

PULLED PORK IN BBQ SAUCE

Prep time: **15 minutes** | Cook time: **8 hours** | Serves **8**

- 1.4kg pork shoulder, diced
- 200g onions, chopped
- 3 green peppers, chopped
- 45g soft brown sugar
- 20ml white wine vinegar
- 170g tomato purée
- 1½ tablespoons chilli powder
- 1 teaspoon English mustard powder
- 2 teaspoons Worcestershire sauce
- 2 teaspoons salt

1. Combine all ingredients in crockpot.
2. Cover and cook on High for 8 hours.
3. Shred meat with forks and mix into sauce. Heat through.
4. Serve in soft bread rolls with grated cheese and coleslaw.

RED MEATS

SPICY SHREDDED BEEF ROLLS

Prep time: 10 minutes | Cook time: 8 hours | Serves 2

- 1 onion, chopped
- 4 garlic cloves, finely chopped
- 2 green chillies, finely chopped
- 700g beef chuck
- 45ml BBQ sauce
- 2 tablespoons clear honey
- 2 tablespoons Dijon mustard
- ½ teaspoon salt
- ⅛ teaspoon cayenne pepper
- 2-3 ciabatta rolls, split and toasted
- 45g round lettuce leaves

1. Layer onion, garlic and chillies in crockpot. Place beef on top.
2. Mix BBQ sauce, honey, mustard, salt and cayenne. Pour over beef.
3. Cover and cook on Low for 8 hours.
4. Remove beef, shred, then return to sauce and stir.
5. Serve in toasted rolls with lettuce.

TENDER PORK JOINT

Prep time: 10 minutes | Cook time: 3-8 hours | Serves 8

- 1.4kg boneless pork joint, cut in half
- 225g passata
- 65ml light soy sauce
- 45g caster sugar
- 2 teaspoons English mustard powder

1. Place roast in crockpot.
2. Combine remaining ingredients in a bowl. Pour over roast.
3. Cover and cook on Low 6-8 hours, or on High 3-4 hours, or until meat is tender but not dry.
4. Remove roast from crockpot to a serving platter. Discard juices or thicken for gravy.

KOREAN-STYLE PULLED PORK WITH KIMCHI

Prep time: 10 minutes | Cook time: 8 hours on low | Serves 2

- 2 tablespoons light soy sauce
- 2 tablespoons soft brown sugar
- 2 teaspoons fresh root ginger, finely chopped
- 2 garlic cloves, finely chopped
- ⅛ teaspoon freshly ground black pepper
- 700g boneless pork shoulder, trimmed
- 145g kimchi
- 20ml chicken stock

1. Mix soy sauce, sugar, ginger, garlic and pepper in a small bowl.
2. Spread mixture over pork in the crockpot.
3. Add kimchi and stock.
4. Cover and cook on Low for 8 hours.
5. Remove pork and shred with two forks.
6. Return meat to cooking liquor, stir and serve.

PORK JOINT WITH POTATOES AND ONIONS

Prep time: 15 minutes | Cook time: 8½ hours | Serves 6-8

- 1.1-1.4kg boneless pork loin joint
- 1 large garlic clove, cut into slivers
- 5-6 potatoes, diced
- 1 large onion, sliced
- 65ml stock, passata or water
- 1½ tablespoons light soy sauce
- 1 tablespoon cornflour
- 1 tablespoon cold water

1. Make small incisions in joint and insert garlic slivers. Brown under grill.
2. Layer half the potatoes and onions in crockpot. Place pork on top, then remaining vegetables.
3. Mix stock and soy sauce, pour over.
4. Cover and cook on Low for 8 hours. Remove meat and vegetables.
5. Mix cornflour with water. Stir into cooking liquor, turn to High and cook until thickened. Serve over carved meat and vegetables.

CHAPTER 5

BBQ-STYLE BEEF JOINT

Prep time: **15-20 minutes** | Cook time: **6-7 hours** | Serves **8**

- 1.8kg beef joint
- 100g tomato ketchup
- 1 onion, chopped
- 65ml water
- 3 tablespoons Worcestershire sauce
- 65g soft brown sugar

1. Place roast in crockpot.
2. In a small bowl, mix together all remaining ingredients except the brown sugar. Pour over roast.
3. Cover and cook on Low 6-7 hours. Approximately 1 hour before serving, sprinkle with 65g brown sugar.

ORANGE AND CRANBERRY PORK JOINT

Prep time: **10 minutes** | Cook time: **8-10 hours** | Serves **6-8**

- 1.4-1.8kg pork joint
- Salt and freshly ground black pepper
- 100g cranberries, finely chopped
- 20g clear honey
- 1 orange, finely grated zest
- ⅛ teaspoon ground cloves
- ⅛ teaspoon ground nutmeg

1. Season joint with salt and pepper. Place in crockpot.
2. Combine remaining ingredients and pour over pork.
3. Cover and cook on Low for 8-10 hours.

SPICED PORK TACOS WITH MOLE SAUCE

Prep time: **10 minutes** | Cook time: **7 to 8 hours** | Serves **4**

- 400g passata
- 100g raisins
- 2 tablespoons chilli powder
- 2 tablespoons ground cumin
- 1 tablespoon chipotle chilli in adobo sauce, finely chopped
- 3 garlic cloves, peeled
- 900g pork shoulder, trimmed and cut into 4cm pieces
- Salt and freshly ground black pepper
- 45g fresh basil, finely chopped
- Juice of 2 limes
- 12 small soft tortillas, warmed

1. Combine passata, raisins, chilli powder, cumin, chipotle and garlic in crockpot. Season pork with salt and pepper, add to cooker. Cook until tender, 7-8 hours on Low or 4-5 hours on High.
2. Remove pork with slotted spoon and shred using two forks. Keep warm.
3. Blend cooking liquid until smooth. Adjust consistency with hot water if needed. Stir in basil and lime juice, season to taste.
4. Toss pork with 100ml sauce. Serve in tortillas with remaining sauce separately.

RED MEATS

HAM AND CHEESE PASTA BAKE

Prep time: 15-30 minutes | Cook time: **2-4 hours** | Serves **8-10**

- 350-450g medium egg pasta
- 1 tin (295g) condensed cream of celery soup
- 600ml soured cream
- 200g cooked ham, diced
- 200g Cheddar cheese, grated

1. Cook pasta according to packet instructions. Drain well.
2. Mix soup and soured cream until smooth. Set aside.
3. Grease the crockpot. Layer one-third each of cooked pasta, ham and cheese.
4. Top with one-quarter of the soup mixture.
5. Repeat layering twice more, finishing with remaining soup mixture.
6. Cook on Low for 2-4 hours, until heated through.

HERBED PORK FILLETS

Prep time: 25 minutes | Cook time: **3-5 hours** | Serves **6-8**

- 45g celery, sliced
- 125g fresh mushrooms, quartered
- 1 medium onion, sliced
- 20g butter, melted
- 2 pork fillets (about 550g each)
- 1 tablespoon butter
- 2 teaspoons salt
- ¼ teaspoon freshly ground black pepper
- 1 tablespoon butter
- 45ml beef stock
- 1 tablespoon plain flour

1. Place celery, mushrooms, onion and 20g melted butter in crockpot.
2. Brown pork in frying pan with 1 tablespoon butter. Place over vegetables.
3. Season with salt and pepper.
4. Mix stock and flour until smooth. Pour over pork.

CHEESY HAM AND MASH BAKE

Prep time: 30-40 minutes | Cook time: **3-4 hours** | Serves **12-16**

- 400g cooked ham, diced
- 60g butter
- 45g onions, chopped
- 1 tablespoon Worcestershire sauce
- 2 tins (400g each) condensed cream of mushroom soup
- 100ml whole milk
- 200g mild Cheddar cheese, diced
- 2.5kg mashed potatoes
- 600ml soured cream
- 6 rashers streaky bacon, grilled and crumbled

1. Sauté ham, butter, onions and Worcestershire sauce in pan until onions are soft. Transfer to large crockpot (or divide between two).
2. Heat soup, milk and cheese in pan until melted. Pour into cooker(s).
3. Mix potatoes with soured cream and spread over top.
4. Sprinkle with crispy bacon.
5. Cover and cook on Low for 3-4 hours, until cheese mixture bubbles up through potato layer.
6. Cover and cook on High for 3 hours, or Low for 4-5 hours.

CHAPTER 5

SAUERKRAUT WITH TWO MEATS

Prep time: **15 minutes** | Cook time: **8-10 hours** | Serves **10**

- 450g braising steak, trimmed
- 450g pork shoulder, trimmed and diced
- 2 tins (295g each) reduced-fat cream of mushroom soup
- 1 packet dry onion soup mix
- 750g sauerkraut
- 200ml skimmed milk
- 350g egg noodles

1. Combine all ingredients except noodles in crockpot.
2. Cook on Low for 8-10 hours.
3. Either add uncooked noodles 2 hours before serving, or cook noodles separately and stir in 15 minutes before serving.

BEEF AND GRAVY

Prep time: **25 minutes** | Cook time: **6-8 hours** | Serves **8**

- 1 onion, chopped
- 15g butter
- 1.4-1.8kg braising steak, cut into 3cm chunks
- 1 teaspoon salt
- ¼ teaspoon freshly ground black pepper
- 200ml water
- 3 beef stock cubes
- 45g plain flour
- To serve:
- Cooked egg pasta or mashed potatoes

1. Melt butter in a large frying pan and cook onion until golden brown. Transfer to crockpot using a slotted spoon, keeping pan juices.
2. Brown meat in batches in the same pan. Transfer to crockpot, reserving pan juices.
3. Make the gravy: Crumble stock cubes into water, then whisk in flour. Add to pan juices and cook, stirring constantly, until thickened. Pour over meat.
4. Cover and cook on Low for 6-8 hours, until meat is tender.
5. Serve over cooked egg pasta or with mashed potatoes.

HERBED PORK FILLET WITH MEDITERRANEAN VEGETABLES

Prep time: **10 minutes** | Cook time: **1 to 2 hours** | Serves **4**

- 450g aubergine, cut into 1cm pieces
- 450g courgettes, cut into 1cm pieces
- 1 onion, chopped
- 2 tablespoons extra virgin olive oil
- 3 garlic cloves, finely chopped
- 1 tablespoon tomato purée
- 1 teaspoon fresh thyme or ¼ teaspoon dried
- Salt and freshly ground black pepper
- 1 tin (400g) chopped tomatoes
- 2 pork fillets (350-450g each), trimmed
- 20g fresh basil, chopped

1. Position oven shelf 15cm from grill element and preheat grill. Toss aubergine, courgettes and onion with 1 tablespoon oil, garlic, tomato purée, thyme, ¼ teaspoon salt and pepper. Spread on foil-lined baking tray and grill until softened and lightly browned, 8-10 minutes. Transfer to crockpot.
2. Add tomatoes to cooker. Season pork and nestle into vegetables, alternating thick and thin ends. Cover and cook on Low until pork reaches 63°C, 1-2 hours.
3. Rest pork under foil for 5 minutes. Stir basil and remaining oil into vegetables, season to taste. Slice pork and serve with vegetables.

CHAPTER 6: FISH AND SEAFOOD

CHAPTER 6

SOY-GINGER STEAMED FISH

Prep time: **5 minutes** | Cook time: **1 hour** | Serves **4**

- 1 whole sea bream or sea bass, cleaned and scaled
- 1 bunch spring onions, finely chopped
- 1 bunch basil, chopped
- 3 teaspoons garlic, finely chopped
- 1 tablespoon fresh root ginger, grated
- 1 tablespoon sweetener of choice
- 60ml light soy sauce
- 60ml dry white wine
- 60ml toasted sesame oil

1. Place spring onions in crockpot and lay fish on top.
2. Whisk together remaining ingredients except basil and pour over fish.
3. Cover and cook on High for 1 hour or until fish is cooked through.
4. Garnish with basil before serving.

TUNA AND PASTA BAKE

Prep time: **10 minutes** | Cook time: **2-8 hours** | Serves **8**

- 100g dried pasta shapes
- 1 teaspoon salt
- 120g onion, finely chopped
- 1 tin (160g) tuna in water, drained
- 1 tin (295g) condensed cream of mushroom soup
- 150ml water
- 25g flaked almonds (optional)
- 120g Gruyère or mature Cheddar, grated
- 150g frozen peas

1. Combine all ingredients except peas in crockpot.
2. Cover and cook on High for 2-3 hours, or Low for 6-8 hours, stirring occasionally.
3. Add peas 20 minutes before end of cooking time. If cooking on High, reduce to Low.

CAJUN PRAWNS WITH GRITS

Prep time: **20 minutes** | Cook time: **3 hours** | Serves **4-6**

- 500g large raw prawns, peeled and deveined
- 100g quick-cooking polenta
- 400ml chicken stock
- 1 onion, diced
- 1 green pepper, diced
- 3 garlic cloves, finely chopped
- 1 tin (400g) chopped tomatoes
- 2 teaspoons Cajun seasoning
- Salt and freshly ground black pepper
- Spring onions, chopped, to garnish

1. Combine all ingredients except spring onions in crockpot.
2. Cover and cook on Low for 3 hours.
3. Serve garnished with spring onions.

CREAMY TUNA PASTA BAKE

Prep time: **10 minutes** | Cook time: **4 hours** | Serves **6**

- 500g dried egg pasta
- 1 medium onion, finely chopped
- 120g mushrooms, sliced
- 180ml chicken stock
- 180ml double cream
- ½ teaspoon sea salt, plus extra to taste
- ½ teaspoon freshly ground black pepper, plus extra to taste
- 2 tins (140g each) tuna in water, drained
- 120g Gruyère cheese, grated
- 250g frozen peas

1. Lightly oil crockpot. Add pasta, onion, mushrooms, stock, cream, salt, pepper and tuna. Stir well.
2. Cover and cook on Low for 4 hours, stirring hourly to prevent sticking.
3. Add cheese and peas for final 20 minutes until cheese melts. Season to taste.

FISH AND SEAFOOD

CHICKEN AND PRAWN JAMBALAYA

Prep time: **15 minutes** | Cook time: **2¼-3¾ hours** | Serves **5-6**

- 1.6-1.8kg chicken, jointed
- 3 onions, diced
- 1 carrot, sliced
- 3-4 garlic cloves, finely chopped
- 1 teaspoon dried oregano
- 1 teaspoon dried basil
- 1 teaspoon salt
- ⅛ teaspoon white pepper
- 1 tin (400g) chopped tomatoes
- 450g raw prawns, peeled
- 400g long-grain rice, cooked

1. Combine all ingredients except prawns and rice in crockpot.
2. Cover and cook on Low for 2-3½ hours until chicken is tender.
3. Add prawns and cooked rice.
4. Cover and cook on High for 15-20 minutes until prawns are pink and cooked through.

ITALIAN FISH STEW

Prep time: **20 minutes** | Cook time: **4 hours** | Serves **6-8**

- 500g mixed seafood (mussels, clams, prawns, white fish)
- 1 onion, diced
- 3 garlic cloves, finely chopped
- 1 tin (400g) chopped tomatoes
- 100ml red wine
- 200ml fish or vegetable stock
- 1 teaspoon dried oregano
- 1 teaspoon dried basil
- ½ teaspoon dried chilli flakes
- Salt and freshly ground black pepper
- Fresh flat-leaf parsley, to garnish

1. Combine all ingredients except parsley in crockpot.
2. Cover and cook on Low for 4 hours.
3. Garnish with parsley before serving.

TUNA AND STUFFING LOAF

Prep time: **5 minutes** | Cook time: **1 hour** | Serves **4**

- 1 tin (295g) condensed cream of mushroom soup, divided
- 180ml whole milk, divided
- 2 eggs, beaten
- 200g sage and onion stuffing mix
- 1 tin (160g) tuna in water, drained and flaked

1. Reserve one-third of soup and 80ml milk. Mix together and set aside.
2. Lightly grease crockpot. Combine remaining ingredients and mix well.
3. Cover and cook on High for 1 hour. Rest for 15 minutes.
4. Meanwhile, heat reserved sauce and serve over the loaf.

LEMON AND DILL SALMON

Prep time: **15 minutes** | Cook time: **2-3 hours** | Serves **4**

- 4 salmon fillets
- 50ml olive oil
- 2 tablespoons fresh dill, chopped
- 2 tablespoons Dijon mustard
- 2 tablespoons clear honey
- Juice of 1 lemon
- Salt and freshly ground black pepper

1. Whisk together oil, dill, mustard, honey, lemon juice, salt and pepper.
2. Place salmon in crockpot and pour over marinade.
3. Cover and cook on Low for 2-3 hours until salmon is cooked through.

CHAPTER 6

CRAB PASTA SAUCE

Prep time: **15 minutes** | Cook time: **4-6 hours** | Serves **4-6**

- 1 medium onion, chopped
- 225g chestnut mushrooms, sliced
- 2 tins (400g each) passata or 1 tin passata and 1 tin chopped tomatoes
- 200g tomato purée
- ½ teaspoon garlic powder
- ½ teaspoon dried basil
- ½ teaspoon dried oregano
- ½ teaspoon salt
- 450g white crabmeat
- 450g fine spaghetti, cooked

1. Soften onions and mushrooms in non-stick frying pan. Transfer to crockpot.
2. Add passata, purée, seasonings and crab. Stir well.
3. Cover and cook on Low for 4-6 hours.
4. Serve over cooked spaghetti.

MEDITERRANEAN-STYLE COD

Prep time: **15 minutes** | Cook time: **2-3 hours** | Serves **4**

- 4 cod fillets
- 1 tin (400g) chopped tomatoes
- 80g black olives, pitted and sliced
- 50g capers
- 2 garlic cloves, finely chopped
- 1 teaspoon dried oregano
- 1 teaspoon dried basil
- Salt and freshly ground black pepper
- Feta cheese, crumbled, to garnish

1. Combine all ingredients except feta in crockpot.
2. Cover and cook on Low for 2-3 hours until cod flakes easily.
3. Serve garnished with crumbled feta.

SPICY PRAWN TACOS

Prep time: **10 minutes** | Cook time: **6 to 7 hours** | Serves **4 to 6**

- 4 green chillies, deseeded and cut into strips
- 3 onions, halved and thinly sliced
- 3 tablespoons extra virgin olive oil
- 4 garlic cloves, thinly sliced
- ½ teaspoon dried oregano
- Salt and freshly ground black pepper
- 680g large raw prawns, peeled and cut into 2.5cm pieces
- 2 tablespoons fresh basil, finely chopped
- 1 lime, zest and juice
- 12-18 small soft tortillas, warmed

1. Mix chillies and onions with 2 tablespoons oil, garlic, oregano, ½ teaspoon salt and pepper in crockpot. Cook until tender, 6-7 hours on Low or 4-5 hours on High.
2. Season prawns and add to cooker. Cook on High for 30-40 minutes until pink.
3. Drain mixture and return to cooker. Stir in basil, lime zest and juice, and remaining oil. Season to taste.
4. Serve in warm tortillas.

CLASSIC FISH STEW

Prep time: **20 minutes** | Cook time: **4 hours** | Serves **6**

- 500g white fish fillets (cod, haddock or pollock), cut into chunks
- 1 onion, diced
- 2 carrots, sliced
- 2 celery sticks, chopped
- 3 garlic cloves, finely chopped
- 1 tin (400g) chopped tomatoes
- 750ml fish or vegetable stock
- 1 teaspoon dried thyme
- 1 teaspoon dried rosemary
- Salt and freshly ground black pepper
- 80g frozen peas (optional)

1. Combine all ingredients except peas in crockpot.
2. Cover and cook on Low for 4 hours.
3. If using, add peas for final 30 minutes.
4. Serve hot.

FISH AND SEAFOOD

COCONUT AND LIME PRAWN CURRY

Prep time: 20 minutes | Cook time: 3 hours | Serves 4-6

- 500g large raw prawns, peeled and deveined
- 1 tin (400ml) coconut milk
- 1 red pepper, sliced
- 1 yellow pepper, sliced
- 1 onion, thinly sliced
- 3 garlic cloves, finely chopped
- 1 tablespoon Thai red curry paste
- 2 tablespoons fish sauce
- 2 tablespoons light soy sauce
- Juice of 2 limes
- Fresh basil leaves, to garnish
- Cooked jasmine rice, to serve

1. Mix coconut milk, curry paste, fish sauce, soy sauce and lime juice in crockpot.
2. Add prawns, peppers, onion and garlic. Stir to combine.
3. Cover and cook on Low for 3 hours.
4. Serve over rice, garnished with basil.

WINE-POACHED SALMON

Prep time: 15 minutes | Cook time: 2 hours | Serves 4

- 450ml water
- 240ml dry white wine
- 1 lemon, thinly sliced
- 1 small mild onion, thinly sliced
- 1 bay leaf
- Mixed fresh herbs (tarragon, dill and parsley)
- 1kg salmon fillet, skin on
- 1 teaspoon salt
- 1 teaspoon freshly ground black pepper

1. Place all ingredients except salmon and seasoning in crockpot. Cook on Low for 1 hour.
2. Season salmon and place skin-side down in cooking liquid.
3. Cook on Low for 1 hour more.

THAI COCONUT SEAFOOD SOUP

Prep time: 20 minutes | Cook time: 3 hours | Serves 4-6

- 500g mixed seafood (prawns, mussels, squid)
- 1 tin (400ml) coconut milk
- 400ml fish stock
- 2 tablespoons Thai red curry paste
- 2 tablespoons fish sauce
- 1 tablespoon soft brown sugar
- 1 red pepper, sliced
- 1 carrot, cut into matchsticks
- 1 courgette, sliced
- Juice of 2 limes
- Fresh Thai basil, to garnish

1. Combine coconut milk, stock, curry paste, fish sauce and sugar in crockpot.
2. Add seafood and vegetables.
3. Cover and cook on Low for 3 hours.
4. Stir in lime juice before serving. Garnish with Thai basil.

GARLIC AND HERB BUTTER PRAWNS

Prep time: 15 minutes | Cook time: 2 hours | Serves 4

- 500g large raw prawns, peeled and deveined
- 80g unsalted butter, melted
- 4 garlic cloves, finely chopped
- 2 tablespoons fresh flat-leaf parsley, finely chopped
- 1 teaspoon dried thyme
- Sea salt and freshly ground black pepper
- 1 lemon, thinly sliced

1. In the crockpot, combine the melted butter, garlic, parsley, thyme, and a good pinch each of salt and pepper.
2. Add the prawns and toss gently until evenly coated.
3. Arrange the lemon slices over the top.
4. Cover and cook on low for 2 hours, or until the prawns are pink and cooked through.
5. Check seasoning before serving.

CHAPTER 6

TERIYAKI SALMON

Prep time: **15 minutes** | Cook time: **2-3 hours** | Serves **4**

- 4 salmon fillets
- 80ml light soy sauce
- 50g soft brown sugar
- 3 tablespoons rice wine vinegar
- 2 tablespoons toasted sesame oil
- 2 garlic cloves, finely chopped
- 1 tablespoon fresh root ginger, grated
- Sesame seeds and spring onions, to garnish

1. Whisk together soy sauce, sugar, vinegar, sesame oil, garlic and ginger.
2. Place salmon in crockpot and pour over sauce.
3. Cover and cook on Low for 2-3 hours until cooked through.
4. Garnish with sesame seeds and spring onions.

COURGETTE AND PRAWN GRATIN

Prep time: **5 minutes** | Cook time: **2 hours** | Serves **6**

- 450g raw prawns, peeled and deveined
- 2 courgettes, cut into 2cm chunks
- 200g cherry tomatoes, halved
- 150g mozzarella, grated
- 4 tablespoons full-fat soft cheese
- 1 tablespoon butter, melted
- 1 teaspoon sea salt
- 1 tablespoon passata
- 175ml water

1. In the crockpot, combine the prawns, courgettes, tomatoes, melted butter, salt, passata and water. Mix gently.
2. Dot the soft cheese over the top and sprinkle with mozzarella.
3. Cover and cook on high for 2 hours, or until the prawns are cooked through and the cheese is melted and bubbling.

MOROCCAN FISH TAGINE

Prep time: **10 minutes** | Cook time: **7 to 8 hours** | Serves **4 to 6**

- 2 onions, finely chopped
- 2 tablespoons tomato purée
- 4 garlic cloves, finely chopped
- 1 tablespoon vegetable oil
- 2 teaspoons garam masala
- 1½ teaspoons paprika
- ¼ teaspoon cayenne pepper
- 400g jar artichoke hearts, halved and drained
- 500ml chicken stock
- 1 tin (400g) chopped tomatoes, drained
- 60ml dry white wine
- Salt and freshly ground black pepper
- 680g skinless cod fillets, cut into 5cm pieces
- 120g Kalamata olives, roughly chopped
- 2 tablespoons fresh flat-leaf parsley, finely chopped

1. Microwave onions, tomato purée, garlic, oil and spices, stirring occasionally, until onions soften (about 5 minutes). Transfer to crockpot with artichokes, stock, tomatoes, wine and ½ teaspoon salt.
2. Cover and cook on Low for 7-8 hours or High for 4-5 hours.
3. Add cod and olives. Cook on High for 30-40 minutes until fish flakes easily.
4. Stir in parsley and season to taste.

FISH AND SEAFOOD

LIME COD AND PRAWNS

Prep time: **5 minutes** | Cook time: **3 hours** | Serves **4**

- 450g cod fillet, skinless and cut into 3cm chunks
- 225g raw prawns, peeled and deveined
- Juice of 1 lime
- 1 teaspoon mixed herbs
- 1 teaspoon dried rosemary
- ⅓ teaspoon cayenne pepper
- ½ teaspoon ground ginger
- ¾ teaspoon ground cinnamon
- 15g butter

1. Place the cod and prawns in the crockpot. Add the lime juice, mixed herbs, rosemary, cayenne pepper, ginger and cinnamon. Gently toss to combine.
2. Dot the butter over the top of the mixture.
3. Cover and cook on high for 3 hours, or until the fish flakes easily and the prawns are pink and cooked through.
4. Season to taste and serve hot in warmed bowls.

MUSSELS IN CREAM

Prep time: **9 minutes** | Cook time: **2 hours** | Serves **2**

- 900g fresh mussels, cleaned and de-bearded
- 30g butter
- 1 medium onion, finely diced
- 1 garlic clove, finely chopped
- ½ teaspoon dried rosemary
- 240ml chicken stock
- 2 tablespoons fresh lemon juice
- 120ml double cream
- Sea salt and freshly ground black pepper

1. Check all mussels are tightly closed, discarding any that remain open when tapped.
2. Place all ingredients except the cream in the crockpot.
3. Cover and cook on high for 2 hours, or until all mussels have opened wide.
4. Remove the lid and stir in the cream gently.
5. Discard any mussels that haven't opened during cooking.
6. Season to taste and serve immediately.

SEAFOOD JAMBALAYA

Prep time: **20 minutes** | Cook time: **4 hours** | Serves **6-8**

- 500g mixed seafood (prawns, mussels, white fish)
- 1 onion, diced
- 1 green pepper, diced
- 3 celery sticks, chopped
- 3 garlic cloves, finely chopped
- 1 tin (400g) chopped tomatoes
- 100ml chicken stock
- 100g long-grain rice
- 2 teaspoons Cajun seasoning
- 1 teaspoon dried thyme
- Sea salt and freshly ground black pepper
- Fresh flat-leaf parsley, chopped, to garnish

1. Place all ingredients except the parsley in the crockpot and stir well to combine.
2. Cover and cook on low for 4 hours, or until the rice is tender and the seafood is cooked through.
3. Before serving, fluff the rice with a fork and check the seasoning.
4. Garnish with the chopped parsley.

SOY AND GINGER BRAISED SQUID

Prep time: **5 minutes** | Cook time: **8 hours** | Serves **6**

- 500g fresh squid, cleaned and cut into rings
- 2 spring onions, finely sliced
- 2 bay leaves
- 1 tablespoon fresh ginger, finely grated
- 1 whole garlic bulb, cloves peeled and finely chopped
- 100g low-calorie granulated sweetener
- 60ml light soy sauce
- 60ml oyster sauce
- 60ml vegetable oil
- 60ml dry white wine

1. Place all ingredients in a 3-litre crockpot and stir gently to combine.
2. Cover and cook on low for 8 hours, or until the squid is tender.
3. Check seasoning before serving.

CHAPTER 6

CHOCOLATE AND CRISPY BACON CUPCAKES

Prep time: **5 minutes** | Cook time: **3 hours** | Makes **10**

For the cupcakes:
- 5 rashers streaky bacon
- 150g dark chocolate (70% cocoa solids)
- 130g ground hazelnuts
- 1 teaspoon baking powder
- 2 medium free-range eggs, lightly beaten
- 120ml full-fat Greek yoghurt
- 1 teaspoon vanilla extract
- Pinch of sea salt

To serve:
- Double cream, whipped
- Extra grated dark chocolate (optional)

1. Cut the bacon into small pieces and fry in a pan until golden and crispy. Drain on kitchen paper and allow to cool completely.
2. Melt the chocolate in a heatproof bowl set over a pan of barely simmering water (don't let the bowl touch the water). Remove from heat and allow to cool slightly.
3. In a medium bowl, combine the ground hazelnuts and baking powder.
4. In a separate bowl, whisk together the eggs, yoghurt, vanilla extract and salt.
5. Fold the wet ingredients into the hazelnut mixture until just combined.
6. Line the base of your crockpot with foil, making a collar around the edges to help lift the cupcakes out later.
7. Place the paper cases in the crockpot (you may need to cook in batches depending on the size of your crockpot).
8. Fill each case two-thirds full with the hazelnut mixture.
9. Mix the crispy bacon pieces into the melted chocolate, then spoon a generous amount over each cupcake.
10. Cover the crockpot with a clean tea towel before putting the lid on (this prevents condensation from dripping onto the cupcakes).
11. Cook on high for 3 hours, or until a skewer inserted into the centre comes out clean.
12. Carefully lift out the cupcakes and cool completely on a wire rack.

HERB-CRUSTED FLOUNDER

Prep time: **5 minutes** | Cook time: **3-4 hours** | Serves **6**

- 900g flounder fillets, skinless
- ½ teaspoon sea salt
- 175ml chicken stock
- 2 tablespoons fresh lemon juice
- 2 tablespoons fresh chives, finely chopped
- 1 small onion, finely diced
- ½-1 teaspoon dried marjoram
- 4 tablespoons fresh flat-leaf parsley, chopped
- Freshly ground black pepper

1. Pat the fish fillets dry thoroughly with kitchen paper. Cut into portions to fit your crockpot if necessary.
2. Season both sides of the fish with sea salt and freshly ground black pepper.
3. In a measuring jug, combine the chicken stock and lemon juice. Add the chives, diced onion, marjoram and half the parsley.
4. Place the rack in your crockpot. If you don't have a rack, scrunch up three long strips of foil into rolls and arrange in the base of the crockpot to elevate the fish.
5. Carefully lay the fish fillets on the rack, trying not to overlap them.
6. Pour the herb and stock mixture evenly over the fish.
7. Cover and cook on high for 3-4 hours, or until the fish flakes easily with a fork.
8. Carefully remove the fish using a fish slice and arrange on warmed plates.
9. Sprinkle with the remaining fresh parsley before serving.

CHAPTER 7: SOUPS AND STEW

CHAPTER 7

CHEESY BACON AND CAULIFLOWER SOUP

Prep time: **15 minutes** | Cook time: **6 hours** | Serves **6**

- 1 tablespoon olive oil
- 400ml chicken stock
- 200ml coconut milk
- 200g cooked chicken, diced
- 100g streaky bacon, cooked and chopped
- 1 medium cauliflower (about 200g), cut into florets
- 1 onion, finely chopped
- 3 garlic cloves, finely chopped
- 50g full-fat soft cheese
- 200g mature Cheddar, grated

1. Lightly grease the crockpot with olive oil.
2. Add stock, coconut milk, chicken, bacon, cauliflower, onion, and garlic.
3. Cover and cook on low for 6 hours.
4. Stir in both cheeses until melted and smooth.

PIZZA SOUP

Prep time: **10 minutes** | Cook time: **5-6 hours** | Serves **6**

- 700ml passata
- 1 x 400g tin chopped tomatoes
- 100g pepperoni, diced (or vegetarian alternative)
- 140g chestnut mushrooms, sliced
- 1 large bell pepper, diced
- 1 large red onion, finely chopped
- 100ml hot water
- 1 tablespoon Italian herbs
- 100g macaroni
- 100g reduced-fat mozzarella, grated

1. Combine all ingredients except cheese in the crockpot.
2. Cover and cook on low for 5-6 hours.
3. Check pasta is tender before serving.
4. Serve in bowls topped with grated mozzarella.

QUICK MINCED BEEF AND VEGETABLE SOUP

Prep time: **15 minutes** | Cook time: **8-9 hours** | Serves **10**

- 500g lean minced beef
- 1L passata or tomato juice
- 500g frozen mixed vegetables
- 200g frozen diced potatoes
- 1 packet onion soup mix

1. Brown the mince in a non-stick frying pan. Drain any excess fat.
2. Transfer to the crockpot and add all remaining ingredients.
3. Cover and cook on low for 8-9 hours.

CLASSIC BEEF AND VEGETABLE SOUP

Prep time: **20-25 minutes** | Cook time: **8-10 hours** | Serves **10-12**

- 1.4kg braising steak, cut into 2.5cm chunks
- 2 tablespoons vegetable oil
- 4 medium potatoes (about 800g), peeled and diced
- 4 carrots, sliced
- 3 celery sticks, sliced
- 2 x 400g tins chopped tomatoes
- 2 medium onions, diced
- ¼ white cabbage, finely sliced
- 2 beef stock cubes
- 2 tablespoons fresh flat-leaf parsley, chopped
- 1 teaspoon mixed herbs
- 1 teaspoon garlic salt
- Freshly ground black pepper
- 750ml-1L hot water

1. Heat the oil in a large frying pan over medium-high heat. Brown the meat in batches until well-coloured. Drain any excess fat.
2. Transfer the meat to your crockpot. Add all remaining ingredients except the water.
3. Pour in enough hot water to just cover the ingredients.
4. Cover and cook on low for 8-10 hours, or until the meat is tender and vegetables are cooked through.

SOUPS AND STEW

SIMPLE VEGETABLE AND MINCE SOUP

Prep time: 20 minutes | Cook time: 8-10 hours | Serves 8-10

- 500g lean minced beef
- 1 large onion, diced
- 1 x 400g tin kidney beans or butter beans
- 3 large carrots, sliced
- 50g long-grain rice
- 2 x 400g tins chopped tomatoes
- 250ml hot water
- 2 beef stock cubes
- 1 tablespoon dried parsley
- 1 teaspoon sea salt
- ¼ teaspoon black pepper
- ¼ teaspoon dried basil
- 1 bay leaf

1. Brown the mince in a frying pan, breaking up any lumps. Drain excess fat.
2. Transfer to the crockpot and add all remaining ingredients.
3. Stir well to combine.
4. Cover and cook on low for 8-10 hours.

CHEDDAR CHEESE AND VEGETABLE SOUP

Prep time: 15 minutes | Cook time: 6 hours | Serves 6

- 15g butter
- 500ml chicken stock
- 100ml coconut milk
- 2 celery sticks, finely diced
- 1 large carrot, finely diced
- 1 onion, finely chopped
- Pinch cayenne pepper
- 225g full-fat soft cheese
- 200g mature Cheddar, grated
- Sea salt and freshly ground black pepper
- 1 tablespoon fresh thyme leaves

1. Grease the crockpot with butter.
2. Add stock, coconut milk, celery, carrot, onion, and cayenne.
3. Cover and cook on low for 6 hours.
4. Stir in both cheeses until melted. Season to taste.
5. Serve garnished with fresh thyme.

CREAMY BEEF AND VEGETABLE SOUP

Prep time: 15 minutes | Cook time: 8-10 hours | Serves 4-6

- 500g lean minced beef
- 1 large onion, chopped
- 330ml vegetable juice (such as V8)
- 2-3 medium potatoes (about 400g), peeled and diced
- 1 tin cream of mushroom soup
- 1 tin cream of celery soup
- 500g frozen mixed vegetables
- 2 teaspoons sea salt
- Freshly ground black pepper

1. Brown the mince with the onions in a frying pan. Drain any excess fat.
2. Transfer to the crockpot and add all remaining ingredients.
3. Stir well to combine.
4. Cover and cook on low for 8-10 hours.

PIZZA-STYLE TACO SOUP

Prep time: 15 minutes | Cook time: 3-4 hours | Serves 8-10

- 900g lean minced beef
- 1 small onion, finely chopped
- ¾ teaspoon sea salt
- Freshly ground black pepper
- 30g taco seasoning mix
- 1L passata
- 1L hot water
- Tortilla chips, to serve
- Mozzarella, grated, to serve
- Soured cream, to serve

1. Brown the mince and onion in a large frying pan. Drain excess fat.
2. Transfer to a large crockpot (minimum 4.5L capacity).
3. Add all remaining ingredients except the toppings.
4. Cover and cook on low for 3-4 hours.

CHAPTER 7

POTATO AND SPINACH SOUP

Prep time: **20 minutes** | Cook time: **8 hours** | Serves **2**

- 400ml vegetable stock
- 2 large Maris Piper potatoes (or other floury potatoes), peeled and diced
- 1 onion, finely chopped
- 45g leeks, finely sliced
- 2 garlic cloves, finely chopped
- ½ teaspoon sea salt
- ½ teaspoon dried marjoram
- Freshly ground black pepper
- 200g baby spinach leaves

1. Combine stock, potatoes, onion, leeks, garlic and seasonings in the crockpot.
2. Cover and cook on low for 7½ hours.
3. Using a stick blender or potato masher, partially blend until desired consistency is reached.
4. Stir in the spinach, cover and cook for a further 20-30 minutes until wilted.

SPICY ITALIAN SAUSAGE AND POTATO SOUP

Prep time: **15-20 minutes** | Cook time: **4-5 hours** | Serves **4**

- 450ml chicken stock
- 45ml double cream
- 3 carrots, coarsely grated
- 4 medium potatoes, peeled and diced
- 400g curly kale, stems removed and roughly chopped
- 450g Italian-style sausages, meat removed from casings and browned
- ½ teaspoon sea salt
- ½ teaspoon dried chilli flakes

1. Combine stock and cream in the crockpot. Set to high.
2. Add prepared vegetables and browned sausage meat.
3. Season with salt and chilli flakes.
4. Cover and cook on high for 4-5 hours, stirring occasionally.

MIXED BEAN AND SAUSAGE STEW

Prep time: **15 minutes** | Cook time: **2-3 hours** | Serves **8**

- 450g pork sausagemeat
- 450g lean minced beef
- 1 x 800g tin baked beans
- 2 x 400g tins kidney beans (light and dark)
- 1 x 400g tin green beans, drained
- 1 x 400g tin butter beans, drained
- 100g tomato ketchup
- 100g dark brown sugar
- 1 tablespoon English mustard

1. Brown sausagemeat and mince separately. Drain excess fat.
2. Combine all ingredients in the crockpot.
3. Cover and cook on high for 2-3 hours.

FRENCH COUNTRY BEAN SOUP

Prep time: **10 minutes** | Cook time: **10 hours** | Serves **8**

- 200g mixed dried beans, soaked overnight
- 2 litres water
- 1 ham hock
- 1 teaspoon sea salt
- Freshly ground black pepper
- 1 x 400g tin chopped tomatoes
- 1 large onion, diced
- 1 garlic clove, finely chopped
- 1 fresh red chilli, deseeded and finely chopped (or 1 teaspoon chilli powder)
- 20ml lemon juice

1. Drain and rinse the pre-soaked beans.
2. Combine all ingredients in the crockpot.
3. Cook on low for 8 hours, then high for 2 hours until beans are tender.
4. Remove ham hock, shred meat and return to soup.

SOUPS AND STEW

SPICY BEAN SOUP

Prep time: **10 minutes** | Cook time: **1½ hours** | Serves **12**

- 350g pork sausagemeat
- 450g extra-lean minced beef
- 1 packet reduced-salt taco seasoning
- 400ml hot water
- 2 x 400g tins kidney beans, drained and rinsed
- 2 x 400g tins chopped tomatoes
- 2 x 400g tins Mexican-style tomatoes
- 450g fresh salsa

1. Brown sausagemeat and mince in a non-stick pan. Transfer to crockpot.
2. Add taco seasoning and mix well.
3. Add remaining ingredients and stir to combine.
4. Cover and cook on high for 1 hour.
5. Remove lid and cook for 30 minutes more, stirring occasionally.

BLACK BEAN AND PORK CHILLI

Prep time: **10 minutes** | Cook time: **6-8 hours** | Serves **8**

- 450g pork tenderloin, cut into 2.5cm chunks
- 450g thick salsa
- 3 x 400g tins black beans, drained and rinsed
- 45ml chicken stock
- 1 red pepper, diced
- 1 onion, finely chopped
- 1 teaspoon ground cumin
- 2-3 teaspoons chilli powder
- 1-1½ teaspoons dried oregano
- Soured cream, to serve

1. Combine all ingredients except soured cream in crockpot.
2. Cover and cook on low for 6-8 hours until pork is tender.
3. Taste and adjust seasoning if needed.
4. Serve with a dollop of soured cream.

MINCED BEEF AND POLISH SAUSAGE SOUP

Prep time: **20-25 minutes** | Cook time: **8-10 hours** | Serves **4-6**

- 450g lean minced beef
- 450g Polish sausage, sliced
- ½ teaspoon mixed herbs
- ¼ teaspoon dried oregano
- ¼ teaspoon dried basil
- 1 packet onion soup mix
- 600ml boiling water
- 1 x 400g tin chopped tomatoes
- 1 tablespoon light soy sauce
- 45g celery, sliced
- 20g celery leaves, chopped
- 100g carrots, peeled and sliced
- 100g macaroni

1. Brown mince and sausage separately. Drain excess fat.
2. Place meat in crockpot with herbs and soup mix.
3. Add hot water, tomatoes, and soy sauce.
4. Add vegetables and stir well.
5. Cover and cook on low for 7-9 hours.
6. Add macaroni for final hour of cooking.

LENTIL AND VEGETABLE SOUP

Prep time: **15 minutes** | Cook time: **8 hours** | Serves **2**

- 45g dried red lentils
- 100g cherry tomatoes, halved
- 2 carrots, diced
- 2 celery sticks, sliced
- 1 onion, finely chopped
- 3 garlic cloves, thinly sliced
- 1 bay leaf
- ½ teaspoon dried thyme
- ½ teaspoon dried marjoram
- ½ teaspoon sea salt
- 200ml vegetable stock
- 100ml water
- 2 tablespoons fresh thyme leaves

1. Rinse the lentils in a fine sieve until water runs clear.
2. Place all ingredients except fresh thyme in the crockpot.
3. Cover and cook on low for 8 hours, or until lentils are tender.
4. Remove bay leaf and stir in fresh thyme before serving.

CHAPTER 7

TUSCAN SAUSAGE AND POTATO SOUP

Prep time: **20-25 minutes** | Cook time: **6-8 hours** | Serves **4-6**

- 2 medium Maris Piper potatoes (or other floury potatoes)
- 450g Italian-style sausages
- 400ml chicken stock
- 200g curly kale, stems removed and roughly chopped
- ½ teaspoon dried chilli flakes (optional)
- 45ml double cream or single cream

1. Peel and dice potatoes into 1cm cubes. Place in crockpot.
2. Remove sausage meat from casings and brown in a frying pan. Slice into 1cm pieces.
3. Add sausage and all remaining ingredients except cream to crockpot.
4. Cover and cook on low for 6-8 hours.
5. Stir in cream 15-20 minutes before serving and heat through.

RUSTIC BEAN AND BACON SOUP

Prep time: **25 minutes** | Cook time: **11-13½ hours** | Serves **6**

- 100g mixed dried beans
- 800ml water, divided
- 1 onion, finely chopped
- 4 rashers smoked back bacon, grilled and crumbled
- 1 packet taco seasoning mix
- 2 x 400g tins chopped tomatoes

1. For the beans:
   - Place dried beans in a large pan with 500ml water
   - Bring to boil, cook for 2 minutes
   - Remove from heat, cover and stand for 1 hour
   - Return to heat and simmer for 2½-3 hours until tender
   - Drain well
2. Place cooked beans, onion, 300ml fresh water, bacon and taco seasoning in crockpot.
3. Cook on low for 8-10 hours.
4. Add tomatoes, stir well and cook for final 30 minutes.

COUNTRY BEAN AND HAM SOUP

Prep time: **45-60 minutes** | Cook time: **4 hours** | Serves **6-8**

- 85g mixed dried beans
- 500ml water
- 1 ham hock
- 100g onions, finely diced
- 100g celery, finely diced
- 100g carrots, finely diced
- 200-300ml additional water
- 1 teaspoon sea salt
- Freshly ground black pepper

- Fresh herbs (or dried equivalent):
- 2 teaspoons fresh basil (or ½ teaspoon dried)
- 2 teaspoons fresh oregano (or ½ teaspoon dried)
- 2 teaspoons fresh thyme (or ½ teaspoon dried)
- 200g fresh tomatoes, chopped (or 1 x 400g tin chopped tomatoes)

1. Combine beans, water and ham hock in a large pan. Bring to boil, turn off heat and stand for 1 hour.
2. Meanwhile, soften vegetables in 200-300ml water until tender. Partially mash.
3. Transfer everything to the crockpot, adding herbs and seasonings.
4. Cook on high for 2 hours, then low for 2 hours.

CHAPTER 8: VEGAN AND VEGETARIAN

CHAPTER 8

CONVENIENT CROCKPOT LASAGNA

Prep time: **30-45 minutes** | Cook time: **4 hours** | Serves **6-8**

- 500g lean minced beef
- 2 x 700g jars passata
- 250g dried lasagne sheets
- 400g mozzarella, grated
- 120g cottage cheese
- Oil spray for greasing

1. Lightly spray the crockpot with oil.
2. Brown the mince in a large frying pan. Drain any excess fat.
3. Stir passata into the mince and mix well.
4. Layer in the crockpot:
   - Quarter of the meat sauce
   - Third of the lasagne sheets (break to fit)
   - Third of the combined cheeses
   - Repeat layers twice
   - Top with remaining sauce
5. Cover and cook on low for 4 hours.

LENTIL RAGU WITH PASTA

Prep time: **15 minutes** | Cook time: **3-10 hours** | Serves **4-6**

For the sauce:
- 45g onion, finely diced
- 45g carrots, finely diced
- 45g celery, finely diced
- 200g chopped tomatoes
- 100g tomato passata
- 100g dried red lentils, rinsed
- ½ teaspoon dried oregano
- ½ teaspoon dried basil
- ½ teaspoon garlic powder
- ¼ teaspoon chilli flakes
- To serve:
- 400g angel hair pasta or spaghetti

1. Combine all sauce ingredients in the crockpot.
2. Cook on low for 8-10 hours or high for 3-5 hours.
3. Cook pasta according to packet instructions just before serving.
4. Toss pasta with the lentil sauce.

INDIAN-STYLE VEGETABLE CURRY

Prep time: **10 minutes** | Cook time: **4 to 5 hours** | Serves **4 to 6**

- 1 onion, finely chopped
- 3 garlic cloves, finely chopped
- 1 tablespoon vegetable oil
- 1 tablespoon fresh ginger, grated
- 1 tablespoon tomato purée
- 1 tablespoon medium curry powder
- ½ teaspoon garam masala
- 400ml vegetable stock, plus extra if needed
- 450g red potatoes, unpeeled and diced
- 400g firm tofu, cut into 1cm cubes
- 1 tablespoon instant tapioca
- 1 x 400ml tin coconut milk
- 200g frozen green beans
- 20g fresh basil, chopped
- Sea salt and freshly ground black pepper

1. Microwave onion, garlic, oil, ginger, tomato purée and spices with ½ teaspoon salt for 5 minutes, stirring occasionally.
2. Transfer to crockpot with stock, potatoes, tofu and tapioca.
3. Cover and cook until potatoes are tender: 4-5 hours on low or 3-4 hours on high.
4. Heat coconut milk in microwave for 3 minutes, stirring occasionally.
5. Stir in coconut milk and beans, leave for 5 minutes.

VEGAN AND VEGETARIAN

VEGETARIAN SLOPPY JOES

Prep time: **20 minutes** | Cook time: **4-5 hours** | Serves **10**

- 100g dried red lentils
- 200ml water
- 100g celery, finely diced
- 100g carrots, finely diced
- 100g onions, finely diced
- 65g tomato ketchup
- 2 tablespoons dark brown sugar
- 2 tablespoons Worcestershire sauce (use vegetarian version if needed)
- 2 tablespoons cider vinegar
- Soft rolls, to serve

1. Pre-cook lentils:
   - Combine lentils and water in a pan
   - Bring to boil, reduce heat
   - Simmer covered for 10 minutes
2. Transfer lentils and cooking water to crockpot.
3. Add all other ingredients except vinegar.
4. Cover and cook on low for 8-10 hours until lentils are tender.
5. Stir in vinegar before serving.
6. Serve on soft rolls (about 45g filling per roll).

TRADITIONAL BEEF BORSCHT

Prep time: **20 minutes** | Cook time: **8-10 hours** | Serves **8**

- 450g cooked beef roast, cut into 2cm cubes
- ½ medium white cabbage, finely sliced
- 3 medium potatoes, peeled and diced
- 4 carrots, sliced
- 1 large onion, diced
- 100g fresh tomatoes, diced
- 100g sweetcorn (fresh or frozen)
- 100g green beans
- 200ml beef stock
- 200ml tomato juice
- ¼ teaspoon garlic powder
- ¼ teaspoon dill seeds
- 2 teaspoons sea salt
- Freshly ground black pepper
- Hot water to cover
- Soured cream, to serve

1. Combine all ingredients except water and soured cream in crockpot.
2. Add enough hot water to fill the crockpot three-quarters full.
3. Cover and cook on low for 8-10 hours.
4. Serve hot with a dollop of soured cream.

CREAMED SPINACH BAKE

Prep time: **10 minutes** | Cook time: **5 hours** | Serves **8**

- 3 x 300g bags frozen spinach, thawed and well drained
- 200g cottage cheese
- 145g mature Cheddar, grated
- 3 medium eggs, beaten
- 20g plain flour
- 1 teaspoon sea salt
- 45g butter, melted

1. Squeeze excess water from spinach thoroughly.
2. Mix all ingredients together well.
3. Transfer to crockpot.
4. Cook on high for 1 hour, then reduce to low for 4 hours.

MEDITERRANEAN BRUSSELS SPROUTS

Prep time: **5 minutes** | Cook time: **6 hours** | Serves **8**

- 900g Brussels sprouts, trimmed and halved if large
- ¼ teaspoon dried oregano
- ½ teaspoon dried basil
- 1 x 50g jar pimentos, drained
- 20g sliced black olives, drained
- 1 tablespoon olive oil
- 45ml hot water

1. Combine all ingredients in the crockpot.
2. Cover and cook on low for 6 hours or until sprouts are tender.

CHAPTER 8

CREAMY BROCCOLI AND CAULIFLOWER BAKE

Prep time: **15 minutes** | Cook time: **6 hours** | Serves **6**

- 1 tablespoon olive oil
- 450g broccoli, cut into florets
- 450g cauliflower, cut into florets
- 25g ground almonds
- 200ml coconut milk
- ½ teaspoon freshly grated nutmeg
- Freshly ground black pepper
- 150g Gouda cheese, grated (divided)

1. Lightly grease the crockpot with olive oil.
2. Layer the broccoli and cauliflower in the cooker.
3. In a bowl, combine ground almonds, coconut milk, nutmeg, pepper and 100g of the cheese.
4. Pour mixture over vegetables and top with remaining cheese.
5. Cover and cook on low for 6 hours.

CLASSIC MACARONI CHEESE

Prep time: **20 minutes** | Cook time: **4¼ hours** | Serves **6-8**

- 450g dried macaroni
- 45g butter
- 2 medium eggs, beaten
- 340ml evaporated milk
- 1 tin condensed cream of cheese soup
- 100ml whole milk
- 400g mature Cheddar, grated (divided)
- ¼ teaspoon paprika

1. Cook macaroni according to packet instructions until just tender. Drain.
2. Transfer hot macaroni to crockpot and add butter. Stir until melted.
3. Mix eggs, evaporated milk, soup, milk and 300g cheese. Pour over macaroni.
4. Cover and cook on low for 4 hours.
5. Top with remaining cheese and cook for 15 minutes more.
6. Dust with paprika before serving.

WILD RICE WITH BACON AND CHERRIES

Prep time: **10 minutes** | Cook time: **6 hours** | Serves **4**

- 1 teaspoon olive oil
- 65g wild rice
- 50g onion, finely chopped
- 1 rasher smoked bacon, cooked and crumbled
- 1 teaspoon fresh rosemary, finely chopped
- 25g dried cherries
- 200ml chicken stock
- Pinch of sea salt

1. Grease the inside of the crockpot with the olive oil.
   - Put all the ingredients into the crockpot and stir them to mix thoroughly.
   - Cover and cook on low for 6 hours until the rice has absorbed all the water and is tender.

LEMON AND HERB PEARL BARLEY

Prep time: **10 minutes** | Cook time: **6 to 8 hours** | Serves **4**

- 1 teaspoon olive oil
- 50g onion, finely chopped
- 2 tablespoons preserved lemon, finely chopped
- 1 teaspoon fresh thyme leaves
- 25g fresh parsley, chopped (divided)
- 65g pearl barley
- 200ml vegetable stock
- Sea salt and freshly ground black pepper
- ½ lemon, cut into wedges

1. Grease crockpot with oil.
2. Combine all ingredients except half the parsley and lemon wedges.
3. Cook on low for 6-8 hours until barley is tender.
4. Garnish with remaining parsley and lemon wedges.

VEGAN AND VEGETARIAN

SWEET AND SOUR SPICED CABBAGE

Prep time: 20 minutes | Cook time: 3-5 hours | Serves 6

- 1 medium red or white cabbage, finely shredded
- 2 onions, chopped
- 4 Bramley apples, peeled and quartered
- 45g raisins
- 20ml lemon juice
- 20ml apple juice or cider
- 3 tablespoons clear honey
- 1 tablespoon caraway seeds
- ⅛ teaspoon ground allspice
- ½ teaspoon sea salt

1. Combine all ingredients in crockpot.
2. Cook on high for 3-5 hours: 3 hours for crunchy texture; 5 hours for softer cabbage.

RICH TWO-CHEESE MACARONI

Prep time: 8-10 minutes | Cook time: 2½ hours | Serves 6

- 115g butter, cubed
- 200g dried macaroni
- 200g mature Cheddar, grated
- 600g cottage cheese
- 240ml boiling water

1. Place butter in crockpot.
2. Add macaroni, 140g Cheddar and cottage cheese. Mix well.
3. Pour over boiling water. Don't stir.
4. Cook on high for 2 hours.
5. Stir and top with remaining cheese.
6. Stand for 10-15 minutes before serving.

QUINOA, BLACK BEAN AND MANGO SALAD

Prep time: 10 minutes | Cook time: 3 to 4 hours | Serves 4 to 6

- 145g white quinoa, rinsed
- 1 green chilli, deseeded and finely chopped
- 3 tablespoons olive oil
- 1 garlic clove, finely chopped
- 1 teaspoon ground cumin
- 1 teaspoon ground coriander
- 165ml hot water
- 1 x 400g tin black beans, drained and rinsed
- Sea salt and freshly ground black pepper
- 2 red peppers, deseeded and diced
- 1 ripe mango, peeled and diced
- 20g fresh basil leaves
- 3 spring onions, finely sliced
- Juice of 2 limes (about 20ml)

1. Lightly grease crockpot with oil.
2. Microwave quinoa, chilli, 1 tablespoon oil, garlic and spices for 3 minutes, stirring occasionally.
3. Transfer to crockpot with water, beans and salt.
4. Cook on low for 3-4 hours or high for 2-3 hours until quinoa is tender.
5. Cool slightly, then combine with remaining ingredients.

CHAPTER 8

ORANGE-GLAZED BABY CARROTS

Prep time: **10 minutes** | Cook time: **4-6 hours** | Serves **6-8**

- 1kg baby carrots
- 20g soft dark brown sugar
- 45ml orange juice
- 15g butter
- ½-¾ teaspoon ground cinnamon (to taste)
- ¼ teaspoon ground nutmeg
- 2 tablespoons cornflour
- 20ml cold water

1. Place carrots, sugar, orange juice, butter and spices in crockpot.
2. Cover and cook on low for 4-6 hours until carrots are tender.
3. Transfer carrots to a serving dish and keep warm.
4. For the glaze:
   - Pour cooking liquid into a small saucepan
   - Bring to the boil
   - Mix cornflour with cold water until smooth
   - Add to pan and boil for 1 minute, stirring constantly
   - Pour over carrots

LIGHT MACARONI CHEESE

Prep time: **15 minutes** | Cook time: **3 hours** | Serves **8**

- 225g dried macaroni
- 1 x 400g tin evaporated milk
- 100ml semi-skimmed milk
- 2 large eggs, lightly beaten
- 400g reduced-fat mature Cheddar, grated
- ¼ teaspoon salt
- ⅛ teaspoon white pepper
- 20g Parmesan, finely grated

1. Cook macaroni until just tender, drain.
2. Lightly grease crockpot.
3. Combine macaroni, milks, eggs, 300g Cheddar and seasonings.
4. Top with remaining cheese.
5. Cook on low for 3 hours.

NAVY BEAN AND BACON SOUP

Prep time: **15 minutes** | Cook time: **7¼-9¼ hours** | Serves **6**

- 65g dried haricot beans
- 200ml cold water (for soaking)
- 8 rashers smoked back bacon, grilled and crumbled
- 2 medium carrots, sliced
- 1 celery stick, sliced
- 1 onion, diced
- 1 teaspoon mixed herbs
- Freshly ground black pepper
- 1.3L chicken stock
- 100ml whole milk

1. Soak beans in cold water overnight.
2. Drain beans and place in crockpot with all ingredients except milk.
3. Cook on low for 7-9 hours until beans are tender.
4. Blend 200g of mixture until smooth and return to pot.
5. Add milk and heat on high for 10 minutes.

CHEESY PIZZA PASTA

Prep time: **20 minutes** | Cook time: **3-4 hours** | Serves **6-8**

- 675g minced beef or Italian sausage meat
- 1 medium onion, chopped
- 1 green pepper, chopped
- 250g rigatoni pasta, cooked
- 200g jar sliced mushrooms, drained
- 85g sliced pepperoni
- 450g jar pizza sauce
- 285g mozzarella cheese, grated
- 285g Cheddar cheese, grated

1. Brown the minced beef and onions in a saucepan. Drain well.
2. Layer half of each ingredient in the crockpot in this order: minced beef and onions, green pepper, pasta, mushrooms, pepperoni, pizza sauce, Cheddar cheese, and mozzarella cheese. Repeat layers.
3. Cover and cook on Low for 3-4 hours.

VEGAN AND VEGETARIAN

CHEESE AND BREAD SOUFFLÉ

Prep time: **15 minutes** | Cook time: **4-6 hours** | Serves **4**

- 14 slices white bread, crusts removed
- 300g mature Cheddar, grated
- 30g butter, melted
- 6 large eggs
- 300ml whole milk, warmed
- 2 teaspoons Worcestershire sauce
- ½ teaspoon sea salt
- Paprika for sprinkling

1. Grease crockpot well.
2. Layer ingredients:
   - Half the torn bread pieces
   - Half the cheese
   - Half the butter
   - Repeat layers
3. Whisk eggs, warm milk, Worcestershire sauce and salt.
4. Pour over bread and cheese, sprinkle with paprika.
5. Cook on low for 4-6 hours.

SPANISH RICE WITH BLACK BEANS

Prep time: **15 minutes** | Cook time: **7 hours** | Serves **2**

- 1 tablespoon olive oil
- 1 onion, finely chopped
- 3 garlic cloves, finely chopped
- 55g brown rice
- 1 green pepper, diced
- 1 x 400g tin black beans, drained and rinsed
- 1 x 400g tin chopped tomatoes
- 55ml vegetable stock
- 2 teaspoons chilli powder
- ½ teaspoon dried oregano

1. Heat oil in a saucepan over medium heat. Add onion and garlic, cooking until softened (about 5 minutes).
2. Add rice and cook for 1 minute, stirring constantly.
3. Transfer to crockpot with remaining ingredients.
4. Cover and cook on low for 6-7 hours until rice is tender.

SUMMER PEARL BARLEY SALAD

Prep time: **10 minutes** | Cook time: **3 to 4 hours** | Serves **4 to 6**

- 100g pearl barley, rinsed
- 3 tablespoons extra virgin olive oil
- 1 teaspoon ground coriander
- 1 tablespoon lemon zest plus 1 tablespoon juice
- Salt and freshly ground black pepper
- 450g courgettes
- 300g cherry tomatoes, halved
- 45g fresh flat-leaf parsley
- 20g natural yoghurt
- 2 tablespoons finely chopped chives
- 1 garlic clove, finely chopped

1. Lightly grease the crockpot bowl with cooking oil spray. In a microwave-safe bowl, heat the barley, 1 tablespoon oil, and coriander, stirring occasionally, until the barley is lightly toasted and fragrant, about 3 minutes. Transfer to the prepared crockpot. Stir in 220ml water, 2 teaspoons lemon zest, and ½ teaspoon salt. Cover and cook until barley is tender, 3 to 4 hours on low or 2 to 3 hours on high.
2. Drain the barley if needed and transfer to a large serving bowl; allow to cool slightly. Using a vegetable peeler or mandoline, slice the courgettes lengthwise into very thin ribbons. Add the courgette ribbons, tomatoes, and parsley to the bowl with the barley and gently toss to combine.
3. In a separate bowl, whisk together the yoghurt, chives, garlic, lemon juice, ¼ teaspoon salt, ¼ teaspoon pepper, remaining 2 tablespoons oil, and remaining 1 teaspoon lemon zest. Add dressing to salad and toss to coat. Season with salt and pepper to taste. Serve.

CHAPTER 8

TEMPEH-STUFFED PEPPERS

Prep time: **20 minutes** | Cook time: **3-8 hours** | Serves **4**

- 115g tempeh, cut into small cubes
- 1 garlic clove, finely chopped
- 1 x 800g tin chopped tomatoes
- 2 teaspoons soy sauce
- 20g onion, finely chopped
- 145g cooked rice
- 55g mature Cheddar, grated
- Tabasco sauce (optional)
- 4 mixed peppers (any colour)
- 20g mature Cheddar, grated (for topping)

1. Steam tempeh for 10 minutes. Mash with garlic, half the tomatoes and soy sauce.
2. Mix in onions, rice, 15g cheese and Tabasco if using.
3. Remove pepper tops and seeds. Stuff with mixture.
4. Arrange in crockpot (3 on bottom, 1 on top). Pour over remaining tomatoes.
5. Cook Low: 6-8 hours or High: 3-4 hours.
6. Top with remaining cheese for final 30 minutes.

QUINOA-STUFFED ONIONS

Prep time: **20 minutes** | Cook time: **7 hours** | Serves **2**

- 3 large Spanish onions
- 2 garlic cloves, finely chopped
- 1 red pepper, diced
- 45g kale, finely chopped
- 45g quinoa, well rinsed
- 120g fresh salsa
- ½ teaspoon dried thyme
- ½ teaspoon sea salt
- Freshly ground black pepper
- 6 tablespoons vegetable stock
- 20ml water
- 55g mature Cheddar, grated

1. Prepare onions:
   - Slice bottom to create flat base
   - Remove centres leaving 1cm shell
   - Reserve centres for other use
2. Combine garlic, pepper, kale, quinoa, salsa, thyme and seasonings.
3. Fill onions with mixture.
4. Pour stock over filling and water around onions in crockpot.
5. Cook on low for 7 hours.
6. Top with cheese and stand covered for 5 minutes.

BRAISED SWISS CHARD WITH SHIITAKE MUSHROOMS

Prep time: **10 minutes** | Cook time: **1 to 2 hours** | Serves **4 to 6**

- 900g Swiss chard, stems finely chopped, leaves cut into 2.5cm pieces
- 115g shiitake mushrooms, stalks removed and caps sliced 6mm thick
- 3 garlic cloves, finely chopped
- 2 teaspoons grated fresh root ginger
- 2 teaspoons toasted sesame oil
- Salt and freshly ground black pepper
- Pinch of dried chilli flakes
- 1 tablespoon rice vinegar
- 1 tablespoon unsalted butter
- 1 teaspoon caster sugar
- 2 tablespoons chopped roasted peanuts
- 2 spring onions, finely sliced

1. Lightly grease the crockpot bowl with cooking oil spray. In a microwave-safe bowl, heat the chard stems, mushrooms, garlic, 1 teaspoon ginger, 1 teaspoon oil, ¼ teaspoon salt, and chilli flakes, stirring occasionally, until vegetables are softened, about 5 minutes. Transfer to the prepared crockpot. Stir in chard leaves, cover, and cook until chard is tender, 1 to 2 hours on high.
2. Stir in vinegar, butter, sugar, remaining ginger, and remaining oil. Season with salt and pepper to taste. (The Swiss chard can be kept on warm setting for up to 2 hours.) Sprinkle with peanuts and spring onions before serving.

VEGAN AND VEGETARIAN

CREAMY SPAGHETTI WITH MINCED BEEF

Prep time: 25 minutes | Cook time: 4-6 hours | Serves 6

- 100g onions, chopped
- 100g green peppers, chopped
- 15g butter
- 800g tin chopped tomatoes
- 115g tin mushrooms, chopped and drained
- 65g tin sliced black olives, drained
- 2 teaspoons dried oregano
- 450g lean minced beef, browned and drained
- 340g spaghetti, cooked and drained
- 295g tin cream of mushroom soup
- 45ml water
- 200g mature Cheddar cheese, grated
- 20g Parmesan cheese, grated

1. In a frying pan, sauté onions and green peppers in butter until tender. Add tomatoes, mushrooms, olives, oregano, and minced beef. Simmer for 10 minutes. Transfer to the crockpot.
2. Add spaghetti and mix well.
3. Combine soup and water. Pour over the mixture. Sprinkle with cheeses.
4. Cover and cook on Low for 4-6 hours.

CHEESY CABBAGE CASSEROLE

Prep time: 20 minutes | Cook time: 4-5 hours | Serves 6

- 1 large white cabbage, roughly chopped
- 200ml water
- 1 tablespoon sea salt
- 20g butter
- 20g plain flour
- ½-1 teaspoon sea salt
- Freshly ground black pepper
- 120ml whole milk
- 120g mature Cheddar, grated

1. Prepare cabbage:
   - Boil in salted water for 5 minutes
   - Drain well and transfer to crockpot
2. Make cheese sauce:
   - Melt butter in saucepan
   - Stir in flour and seasonings
   - Gradually add milk, stirring constantly
   - Cook for 5 minutes until thickened
   - Remove from heat and stir in cheese
3. Pour sauce over cabbage.
4. Cook on low for 4-5 hours.

VEGETARIAN LASAGNE

Prep time: 15 minutes | Cook time: 5 hours | Serves 8

- 700g low-fat tomato pasta sauce
- 45ml water
- 450g low-fat ricotta cheese
- 200g mozzarella cheese, grated, divided
- 65g Parmesan cheese, grated, divided
- 1 large egg
- 2 teaspoons minced garlic
- 1 teaspoon Italian herbs
- 225g pack fresh lasagne sheets

1. Mix pasta sauce and water in a bowl.
2. In a separate bowl, combine ricotta, 45g mozzarella cheese, 45g Parmesan cheese, egg, garlic, and Italian herbs.
3. Spread ¼ of the sauce mixture in the bottom of the crockpot. Top with 1/3 of the lasagne sheets, cutting to fit if needed.
4. Spread 1/3 of the cheese mixture over the pasta, ensuring sheets are completely covered.
5. Repeat these layers twice more.
6. Spread with remaining sauce.
7. Cover and cook on Low for 5 hours.
8. Sprinkle with remaining cheeses. Cover and let stand for 10 minutes until cheese has melted.

CHAPTER 9: DESSERTS

DESSERTS

CHOCOLATE PEANUT BUTTER SPONGE

Prep time: 7 minutes | Cook time: 2-2½ hours | Serves 8-10

- 200g chocolate sponge cake mix
- 45ml water
- 90g smooth peanut butter
- 2 medium eggs
- 45g chopped mixed nuts

1. Place all ingredients in a large mixing bowl. Beat with an electric mixer for 2 minutes.
2. Grease and flour a pudding basin that fits your crockpot. Pour mixture into the basin. Place basin in crockpot.
3. Cover basin with a double layer of baking parchment.
4. Cover crockpot. Cook on High for 2-2½ hours, or until a skewer inserted into the centre comes out clean.
5. Allow to cool before turning out onto a serving plate.

SIMPLE STUFFED APPLES

Prep time: 15-30 minutes | Cook time: 2½-5 hours | Serves 6-8

- 30g sultanas
- 20g caster sugar
- 6-8 medium Bramley apples, cored but unpeeled
- 1 teaspoon ground cinnamon
- 30g butter
- 45ml water

1. Mix sultanas and sugar in a small bowl.
2. Arrange apples in crockpot. Divide sultana mixture between apple cavities.
3. Dust apples with cinnamon and dot with butter.
4. Pour water around edges of crockpot.
5. Cover and cook on Low for 3-5 hours or High for 2½-3½ hours, until tender but still holding shape.
6. Serve warm with ice cream or custard.

VANILLA POD RICE PUDDING

Prep time: 10 minutes | Cook time: 2½-4 hours | Serves 12

- 600ml skimmed milk
- 145g easy-cook rice, uncooked
- 100g caster sugar
- 100g sultanas
- 15g butter, melted
- ½ teaspoon salt
- 1 vanilla pod, split lengthways
- 1 large egg
- ½ teaspoon ground cinnamon
- 225g low-fat crème fraiche

1. In the crockpot, combine milk, rice, sugar, sultanas, butter, and salt. Stir well.
2. Scrape seeds from vanilla pod. Add both seeds and pod to milk mixture.
3. Cover and cook on High for 2½-4 hours, or until rice is tender and most of liquid is absorbed.
4. In a small bowl, whisk the egg. Gradually add 45g of hot rice mixture to egg, whisking constantly.
5. Return egg mixture to crockpot, stirring constantly. Cook for 1 minute while stirring. Remove ceramic pot from crockpot base.
6. Leave to stand for 5 minutes. Stir in cinnamon and crème fraîche. Remove vanilla pod.
7. Serve warm or chilled.

CHAPTER 9

APPLE CRUMBLE

Prep time: **5-10 minutes** | Cook time: **2-3 hours** | Serves **6-8**

For the Filling

- 800g tin apple pie filling, or
- 55g caster sugar
- 120ml water
- 30g cornflour
- 400g cooking apples, peeled and sliced
- ½ teaspoon ground cinnamon
- ¼ teaspoon ground allspice
- For the Crumble
- 65g porridge oats
- 45g soft light brown sugar
- 45g plain flour
- 20g butter, softened

1. If using fresh apples, mix 55g sugar, water, cornflour, apples, cinnamon, and allspice in the crockpot. If using tinned filling, simply add to the crockpot.
2. Mix crumble ingredients until mixture resembles breadcrumbs. Sprinkle over apple mixture.
3. Cover and cook on Low for 2-3 hours.

SEVEN LAYER TRAYBAKE

Prep time: **5-10 minutes** | Cook time: **2-3 hours** | Serves **6-8**

- 20g butter, melted
- 45g digestive biscuit crumbs
- 45g milk chocolate chips
- 45g butterscotch chips
- 45g desiccated coconut
- 45g chopped mixed nuts
- 45g condensed milk

1. In a loaf tin or cake tin that fits your crockpot, layer ingredients in order listed. Do not stir.
2. Cover and cook on High for 2-3 hours, or until set. Remove tin and uncover. Stand for 5 minutes.
3. Carefully turn out onto a plate and cool completely.

LEMON AND POPPY SEED DRIZZLE PUDDING

Prep time: **10-15 minutes** | Cook time: **2-2½ hours** | Serves **8-10**

For the Sponge

- 1 packet lemon and poppy seed cake mix
- 1 medium egg
- 225g low-fat crème fraîche
- 45ml water
- For the Drizzle
- 15g butter
- 65ml water
- 45g caster sugar
- 20ml fresh lemon juice

1. Mix sponge ingredients until well combined. Spread in lightly greased crockpot bowl.
2. For the drizzle, combine ingredients in a small saucepan. Bring to the boil. Pour hot mixture over cake batter.
3. Cover and cook on High for 2-2½ hours until edges are lightly browned. Turn off heat and leave in cooker for 30 minutes with lid slightly ajar.
4. Once cool enough to handle, invert onto a large plate.
5. Allow to cool completely before serving.

STRAWBERRY AND RHUBARB COMPOTE

Prep time: **10 minutes** | Cook time: **6-7 hours** | Serves **8**

- 600g rhubarb, sliced
- 65g caster sugar
- 1 cinnamon stick (optional)
- 45ml white grape juice
- 200g fresh strawberries, hulled and sliced

1. Place rhubarb in crockpot. Sprinkle with sugar. Add cinnamon stick if using and grape juice. Stir well.
2. Cover and cook on Low for 5-6 hours, or until rhubarb is tender.
3. Add strawberries and cook for 1 hour more.
4. Remove cinnamon stick if used. Chill before serving.

DESSERTS

TOFFEE APPLES

Prep time: **15 minutes** | Cook time: **4-6 hours** | Serves **4**

- 4 large Bramley apples
- 45ml apple juice
- 120g soft brown sugar
- 12 cinnamon sweets
- 60g butter
- 8 toffee sweets
- ¼ teaspoon ground cinnamon
- Whipped double cream, to serve

1. Remove a 1cm strip of peel from the top of each apple and place in the crockpot.
2. Pour apple juice over apples.
3. Fill the core of each apple with 30g brown sugar, 3 cinnamon sweets, 15g butter, and 2 toffee sweets. Dust with cinnamon.
4. Cover and cook on Low for 4-6 hours, or until tender.
5. Serve hot with whipped cream.

LEMON RICE PUDDING

Prep time: **10 minutes** | Cook time: **6 hours** | Serves **2**

- 100g pudding rice
- 55g caster sugar
- 400ml whole milk
- 100ml water
- 20ml fresh lemon juice
- 2 teaspoons finely grated lemon zest
- Pinch of salt
- 60g butter, melted

1. Lightly grease the crockpot bowl with cooking spray.
2. Combine all ingredients in the crockpot and stir well.
3. Cover and cook on Low for 6 hours, or until rice is very tender and mixture has thickened.
4. Serve hot.

WHITE WINE POACHED PEARS

Prep time: **10 minutes** | Cook time: **3 to 4 hours** | Serves **6**

- 750ml dry white wine
- 65g caster sugar
- ½ vanilla pod
- 6 strips lemon zest (5cm each)
- 5 sprigs fresh mint
- 3 sprigs fresh thyme
- ½ cinnamon stick
- Pinch of salt
- 6 firm but ripe Conference or Williams pears (225g each), peeled, halved and cored

1. In the crockpot, whisk wine and sugar until sugar dissolves. Split vanilla pod lengthways. Using the tip of a small knife, scrape out seeds. Add pod, seeds, lemon zest, mint, thyme, cinnamon stick, and salt to wine mixture. Arrange pears in crockpot, cover, and cook until tender when pierced with a knife, 3 to 4 hours on Low or 2 to 3 hours on High.
2. Using a slotted spoon, transfer pears to a shallow serving dish. Strain cooking liquid into a large saucepan. Simmer over medium heat until reduced and syrupy. Pour sauce over pears, cover, and refrigerate until thoroughly chilled, at least 2 hours or up to 3 days. Serve.

DOUBLE CHOCOLATE BREAD AND BUTTER PUDDING

Prep time: **25 minutes** | Cook time: **3 hours** | Serves **2**

- 600g day-old French bread, cubed
- 100g plain chocolate chips
- 200ml chocolate milk
- 4 medium eggs, beaten
- 45g butter, melted
- 45g soft brown sugar
- 20g caster sugar
- 3 tablespoons cocoa powder
- 2 teaspoons vanilla extract

1. Line the crockpot with strong kitchen foil and lightly grease with cooking spray.
2. Place bread cubes and chocolate chips in the crockpot.
3. In a large bowl, beat remaining ingredients together. Pour over bread mixture.
4. Press bread beneath the liquid and leave to soak for 20 minutes.
5. Cover and cook on Low for 3 hours, or until set and reaches 71°C on a cooking thermometer.

CHAPTER 9

CHOCOLATE POTS DE CRÈME

Prep time: **10 minutes** | Cook time: **3 hours** | Serves **6**

- 6 egg yolks
- 200ml double cream
- 20g cocoa powder
- 1 tablespoon vanilla extract
- ½ teaspoon liquid stevia
- Whipped coconut cream, to serve (optional)
- Grated dark chocolate, to serve (optional)

1. Whisk together egg yolks, cream, cocoa powder, vanilla, and stevia in a medium bowl.
2. Pour mixture into a 1.4-litre ovenproof dish and place in the crockpot.
3. Pour hot water around the dish to reach halfway up its sides.
4. Cover and cook on Low for 3 hours.
5. Remove dish and cool to room temperature on a wire rack.
6. Chill completely before serving, topped with whipped coconut cream and grated chocolate if desired.

SPICED FRUIT COMPOTE

Prep time: **10 minutes** | Cook time: **8-10 hours** | Serves **8-10**

- 1 tin peach halves in juice
- 1 tin apricot halves in juice
- 1 tin pear halves in juice
- 1 large tin pineapple chunks in juice
- 1 tin black cherries in juice
- 45g soft brown sugar
- 1 teaspoon curry powder
- 3-4 tablespoons quick-cooking tapioca
- 30g butter (optional)

1. *Combine fruit and leave to stand for 2-8 hours to meld flavours. Drain and transfer to crockpot.*
2. *Add remaining ingredients and mix well. Dot with butter if using.*
3. *Cover and cook on Low for 8-10 hours.*
4. *Serve warm or at room temperature.*

TEA-POACHED PEARS

Prep time: **10 minutes** | Cook time: **3 to 4 hours** | Serves **6**

- 300ml boiling water
- 4 English breakfast tea bags
- 1 cinnamon stick
- 2 star anise
- Pinch of salt
- 20g soft dark brown sugar
- 6 firm but ripe Conference pears (225g each), peeled, halved and cored
- 65g Greek-style yoghurt
- 45g icing sugar
- 15ml Grand Marnier

1. Add boiling water, tea bags, cinnamon stick, star anise, and a pinch of salt to the crockpot. Let steep for 8 minutes, then remove tea bags. Whisk in brown sugar until dissolved. Arrange pears in crockpot, cover, and cook until tender when pierced with a knife, 3 to 4 hours on Low or 2 to 3 hours on High.
2. Using a slotted spoon, transfer pears to a shallow serving dish. Strain cooking liquid into a saucepan. Simmer over medium heat until reduced to about 100ml, 15 to 20 minutes. Pour sauce over pears, cover, and chill for at least 2 hours or up to 3 days.
3. Whisk yoghurt, icing sugar, Grand Marnier, and a pinch of salt until combined. Serve pears with a dollop of the yoghurt mixture.

DESSERTS

RUM-GLAZED BANANAS

Prep time: **10 minutes** | Cook time: **1 to 2 hours** | Serves **6**

- 45g dark muscovado sugar
- 20ml dark rum
- ½ teaspoon ground cinnamon
- ¼ teaspoon salt
- 3 ripe bananas, peeled and halved lengthways and widthways
- 30g unsalted butter, cut into pieces
- 15ml lemon juice
- 1 litre good-quality vanilla ice cream
- 45g pecan nuts or walnuts, toasted and roughly chopped (optional)

1. Lightly grease the crockpot with cooking spray. Whisk sugar, rum, cinnamon, and salt until sugar dissolves. Place bananas cut side down in the crockpot. Cover and cook until tender when pierced, 1 to 2 hours on High. (Can be kept on Warm setting for up to 1 hour.)
2. Carefully transfer bananas to serving bowls using tongs and a fish slice. Whisk butter and lemon juice into sauce until combined. Serve with ice cream, sauce, and nuts if using.

SCANDINAVIAN FRUIT COMPOTE

Prep time: **5 minutes** | Cook time: **8 hours** | Serves **12**

- 100g dried apricots
- 100g dried apple rings
- 100g dried prunes
- 100g tinned pitted cherries
- 45g quick-cooking tapioca
- 100ml red wine or grape juice
- 300ml water, plus extra if needed
- 45ml orange juice
- 20ml lemon juice
- 1 tablespoon grated orange zest
- 45g soft brown sugar

1. Place apricots, apples, prunes, cherries, tapioca, and wine in crockpot. Cover with water.
2. Cook on Low for at least 8 hours.
3. Before serving, stir in remaining ingredients.
4. Serve warm as a dessert soup or chilled over vanilla ice cream.

APPLE AND CARAMEL PUDDING

Prep time: **15 minutes** | Cook time: **6 hours** | Serves **7-8**

- 2 medium Bramley apples, peeled, cored, and cut into wedges
- 45ml apple juice
- 200g soft caramel sweets
- 5ml vanilla extract
- ⅛ teaspoon ground cardamom
- ½ teaspoon ground cinnamon
- 20g smooth peanut butter
- 7 slices madeira cake
- 1 litre vanilla ice cream

1. In the crockpot, combine apple juice, caramel sweets, vanilla, and spices.
2. Add small dollops of peanut butter and stir to combine.
3. Add apple wedges.
4. Cover and cook on Low for 5 hours.
5. Stir thoroughly.
6. Cover and cook for 1 more hour on Low.
7. Serve 20g warm mixture over each slice of madeira cake, topped with ice cream.

BUTTERSCOTCH APPLE CRUMBLE

Prep time: **10-15 minutes** | Cook time: **5-6 hours** | Serves **6**

- 400g Bramley apples, peeled and sliced
- 55g soft brown sugar
- 45g plain flour
- 45g porridge oats
- 1 packet butterscotch Angel Delight
- 1 teaspoon ground cinnamon
- 45g cold butter, diced

1. Place apples in crockpot.
2. Mix remaining dry ingredients, then rub in butter until mixture resembles breadcrumbs. Sprinkle over apples.
3. Cover and cook on Low for 5-6 hours.
4. Serve with vanilla ice cream or custard.

CHAPTER 9

SPICED FRUIT SAUCE

Prep time: **20 minutes** | Cook time: **3½-4¾ hours** | Makes **600g**

- 3 Bramley apples, peeled and sliced
- 3 Conference pears, peeled and sliced
- 15ml lemon juice
- 45g soft brown sugar
- 45ml maple syrup
- 20g butter, melted
- 45g pecans, roughly chopped
- 20g sultanas
- 2 cinnamon sticks
- 1 tablespoon cornflour
- 30ml cold water

1. Toss apples and pears with lemon juice in crockpot.
2. Mix brown sugar, maple syrup, and butter. Pour over fruit.
3. Add pecans, sultanas, and cinnamon sticks.
4. Cover and cook on Low for 3-4 hours.
5. Mix cornflour with water until smooth. Gradually stir into crockpot.
6. Cover and cook on High for 30-40 minutes, or until thickened.
7. Remove cinnamon sticks. Serve warm over madeira cake or ice cream.

FRUIT AND NUT STUFFED APPLES

Prep time: **25 minutes** | Cook time: **1½-3 hours** | Serves **4**

- 4 large Bramley apples
- 15ml lemon juice
- 20g dried apricots, finely chopped
- 20g walnuts or pecans, chopped
- 45g soft brown sugar
- ½ teaspoon cinnamon
- 30g butter, melted
- 45ml apple juice
- 4 pecan halves, to garnish (optional)

1. Core apples, making a 4cm wide cavity, stopping 1cm from bottom. Peel top 2.5cm of each apple. Brush exposed flesh with lemon juice.
2. Combine apricots, nuts, sugar, and cinnamon. Stir in melted butter. Fill apples evenly with mixture.
3. Pour apple juice into crockpot. Place 2 apples on bottom and 2 above, offset so they don't sit directly on top of each other. Cover and cook on Low for 1½-3 hours until tender.
4. Serve warm or at room temperature, topped with pecan halves if desired.

CHOCOLATE SELF-SAUCING PUDDING

Prep time: **10 minutes** | Cook time: **1 to 2 hours** | Serves **6 to 8**

For the Sponge

- 100g plain flour
- 100g caster sugar
- 45g cocoa powder
- 2 teaspoons baking powder
- ¼ teaspoon salt
- 45ml whole milk
- 60g unsalted butter, melted and cooled
- 1 large egg yolk, at room temperature
- 2 teaspoons vanilla extract
- 45g dark chocolate chips
- For the Sauce
- 45g caster sugar
- 20g cocoa powder
- 100ml boiling water

1. Line crockpot with a foil collar and lightly grease with cooking spray. In a large bowl, whisk together flour, 45g sugar, 20g cocoa, baking powder, and salt. In a separate bowl, whisk milk, melted butter, egg yolk, and vanilla. Stir wet mixture into dry ingredients until just combined. Fold in chocolate chips (mixture will be thick).
2. Spread mixture evenly in prepared crockpot. Mix remaining sugar and cocoa, and sprinkle over top. Slowly pour boiling water over. Do not stir.
3. Cover and cook on High for 1 to 2 hours until pudding is puffed and top is set but centre remains gooey when tested.
4. Remove foil collar. Turn off crockpot and let pudding stand, covered, for 10 minutes before serving.

APPENDIX 1: MEASUREMENT CONVERSION CHART

MEASUREMENT CONVERSION CHART

VOLUME EQUIVALENTS (DRY)

US STANDARD	METRIC (APPROXIMATE)
1/8 teaspoon	0.5 mL
1/4 teaspoon	1 mL
1/2 teaspoon	2 mL
3/4 teaspoon	4 mL
1 teaspoon	5 mL
1 tablespoon	15 mL
1/4 cup	59 mL
1/2 cup	118 mL
3/4 cup	177 mL
1 cup	235 mL
2 cups	475 mL
3 cups	700 mL
4 cups	1 L

VOLUME EQUIVALENTS (LIQUID)

US STANDARD	US STANDARD (OUNCES)	METRIC (APPROXIMATE)
2 tablespoons	1 fl.oz.	30 mL
1/4 cup	2 fl.oz.	60 mL
1/2 cup	4 fl.oz.	120 mL
1 cup	8 fl.oz.	240 mL
1 1/2 cup	12 fl.oz.	355 mL
2 cups or 1 pint	16 fl.oz.	475 mL
4 cups or 1 quart	32 fl.oz.	1 L
1 gallon	128 fl.oz.	4 L

TEMPERATURES EQUIVALENTS

FAHRENHEIT (F)	CELSIUS (C) (APPROXIMATE)
225 °F	107 °C
250 °F	120 °C
275 °F	135 °C
300 °F	150 °C
325 °F	160 °C
350 °F	180 °C
375 °F	190 °C
400 °F	205 °C
425 °F	220 °C
450 °F	235 °C
475 °F	245 °C
500 °F	260 °C

WEIGHT EQUIVALENTS

US STANDARD	METRIC (APPROXIMATE)
1 ounce	28 g
2 ounces	57 g
5 ounces	142 g
10 ounces	284 g
15 ounces	425 g
16 ounces (1 pound)	455 g
1.5 pounds	680 g
2 pounds	907 g

APPENDIX 2: THE DIRTY DOZEN AND CLEAN FIFTEEN

The Dirty Dozen and Clean Fifteen

The Environmental Working Group (EWG) is a nonprofit, nonpartisan organization dedicated to protecting human health and the environment Its mission is to empower people to live healthier lives in a healthier environment. This organization publishes an annual list of the twelve kinds of produce, in sequence, that have the highest amount of pesticide residue-the Dirty Dozen-as well as a list of the fifteen kinds of produce that have the least amount of pesticide residue-the Clean Fifteen.

THE DIRTY DOZEN

- The 2016 Dirty Dozen includes the following produce. These are considered among the year's most important produce to buy organic:

  Strawberries
  Apples
  Nectarines
  Peaches
  Celery
  Grapes
  Cherries
  Spinach
  Tomatoes
  Bell peppers
  Cherry tomatoes
  Cucumbers
  Kale/collard greens
  Hot peppers

- The Dirty Dozen list contains two additional items-kale/collard greens and hot peppers-because they tend to contain trace levels of highly hazardous pesticides.

THE CLEAN FIFTEEN

- The least critical to buy organically are the Clean Fifteen list. The following are on the 2016 list:

  Avocados
  Corn
  Pineapples
  Cabbage
  Sweet peas
  Onions
  Asparagus
  Mangos
  Papayas
  Kiw
  Eggplant
  Honeydew
  Grapefruit
  Cantaloupe
  Cauliflower

- Some of the sweet corn sold in the United States are made from genetically engineered (GE) seedstock. Buy organic varieties of these crops to avoid GE produce.

APPENDIX 3: INDEX

A

almonds 38

apples 9, 11, 18, 29, 31, 55, 61, 65, 66

apricots 14, 65, 66

artichoke hearts 7

aubergine 36

avocado 15

B

beans 7, 55

beef 7, 29, 34, 46, 47, 49, 52, 53, 56

beef brisket 32

beef chuck 33

beef short ribs 31, 32

beef stock 30, 35

blueberries 11

broccoli 27

C

cabbage 55

cauliflower 27, 54

chicken breasts 22, 23, 25, 24, 26, 27

chicken drumsticks 24

chicken stock 24, 26, 33, 46, 47, 48, 54

chicken thighs 22, 26, 27

coconut milk 15, 41

coconut oil 11

cod fillets 40, 42, 43

cornflour 7

E

erythritol 11, 15

F

fish stock 41

flounder fillets 44

G

garam masala 42, 52

grape 62

H

ham 35

hazelnuts 11, 44

L

leeks 17

leek soup mix 9

M

macaroni 54, 56

mango 55

marjoram 9

mayonnaise 7

mushrooms 20, 23, 27, 35, 39, 58

O

oats 15, 17, 19, 62

orange 18

oregano 53

P

passata 34, 46

pear 17, 66

pepperoni 56

pineapple 10, 15, 64

pineapple jam 31

pork 29, 31, 33, 34, 35

pork chops 31

pork sausagemeat 16, 48, 49

pork shoulder 16, 32, 33

prawns 24, 38, 41, 42, 43

protein powder 15

R

rhubarb 62

rum 65

S

salmon fillets 39, 41, 42

salsa 7

squid 43

sultanas 61

sunflower seeds 11

T

tempeh 58

tuna 38, 39

V

vanilla extract 11, 19, 64, 65

vanilla ice cream 65

vegetable juice 47

vegetable stock 48, 54, 58

W

white fish fillets 40

Worcestershire sauce 32

Hey there!

Wow, can you believe we've reached the end of this culinary journey together? I'm truly thrilled and filled with joy as I think back on all the recipes we've shared and the flavors we've discovered. This experience, blending a bit of tradition with our own unique twists, has been a journey of love for good food. And knowing you've been out there, giving these dishes a try, has made this adventure incredibly special to me.

Even though we're turning the last page of this book, I hope our conversation about all things delicious doesn't have to end. I cherish your thoughts, your experiments, and yes, even those moments when things didn't go as planned. Every piece of feedback you share is invaluable, helping to enrich this experience for us all.

I'd be so grateful if you could take a moment to share your thoughts with me, be it through a review on Amazon or any other place you feel comfortable expressing yourself online. Whether it's praise, constructive criticism, or even an idea for how we might do things differently in the future, your input is what truly makes this journey meaningful.

This book is a piece of my heart, offered to you with all the love and enthusiasm I have for cooking. But it's your engagement and your words that elevate it to something truly extraordinary.

Thank you from the bottom of my heart for being such an integral part of this culinary adventure. Your openness to trying new things and sharing your experiences has been the greatest gift.

Catch you later,

Renee R. Legere

Printed in Great Britain
by Amazon